5.10 B+T 3.69 Sweeringen

JEAN PAUL MARAT

JEAN PAUL MARAT

A STUDY IN RADICALISM

By

LOUIS R. GOTTSCHALK

THE UNIVERSITY OF CHICAGO PRESS

CHICAGO & LONDON

To
PROFESSOR CARL BECKER

THE UNIVERSITY OF CHICAGO PRESS
CHICAGO & LONDON
The University of Toronto Press, Toronto 5, Canada

New Preface © 1967 by The University of Chicago
All rights reserved
Reissued 1967

Library of Congress Catalog Card Number 67-16987

Printed in the United States of America

PREFACE (1967)

What does candor require that a professor emeritus of nearly sixty-eight say about his first full-length book, which was essentially completed when he was less than one third his present age? If he had continued to study and learn during the intervening decades, he would certainly feel obliged to admit that some parts of that book might profitably be expanded, other parts curtailed, and still others rearranged, corrected, or reinterpreted. If he had grown more conservative with the years, he might confess that he found it more difficult than in his youth to claim an empathy with so eccentric a personality as Marat's. If he had become more familiar with depth psychology, he might indicate (or at least betray) a greater preference for psychoanalytic terms in the depiction of that personality. If he had kept up with the literature on his subject, he would recognize that his bibliography might well be supplemented by some titles selected from among the several biographical works on Marat which have appeared since 1927—in French, German, Italian, and particularly (as one would expect of so bitter a critic of his own society) Russian (though, interestingly enough, nothing of scholarly significance in English).[1] And if he had developed a better ear for clichés, irrelevancies, "historiographese," elegant variations, and verbiage, he might feel a bit uneasy about some of his prose, especially after he had learned from a master of style that one of his paragraphs (p. 17) contained some easily expendable words (see Robert Graves, *But It Still Goes On* [New York, 1931], pp. 142-44).

[1] See my "Quelques études récentes sur Marat," *Annales historiques de la Révolution française*, XIII (1936), 97–122; and there have been several biographies since 1936 in foreign languages. There has also been a French translation (Paris, 1929) and an Italian translation (Milan, 1959) of this book.

For all these shortcomings, an old professor might, eschewing false modesty, yet feel a certain pride that a scholarly publishing house has seen fit to reissue his youthful endeavor. The publishers perhaps were not wholly uninfluenced by the renewed interest in Marat roused by the success of Peter Weiss's imaginative drama, *The Persecution and Assassination of Marat as Performed by the Inmates of the Asylum of Charenton under the Direction of the Marquis de Sade* (English translation, 1965). That consideration alone—if, in fact, it was ever entertained—might provide a scholarly justification for the republication of a still valid if old biography of the central figure in Weiss's play; a sober account by a relatively normal young scholar, inmate of an ivory tower, may remind the reader that, histrionic and rabid though Marat was, his life story is comprehensible in sober, academic terms qualified by a studied adherence to the historians' time-honored aspirations toward verity and disinterested judgment.

I have heard that Senator Albert Beveridge once said that the more he learned about Abraham Lincoln, the better he liked Stephen Douglas. I have spent the four decades since the first publication of this book studying the life and times of the Marquis de Lafayette, and the more I learn about Lafayette, the *less* I like Marat. If my preoccupation with my volumes on Lafayette and other historical subjects did not preclude a thorough revision of this book, it is highly likely that my rewriting of it would deal at greater length with the conflict between Lafayette as a champion of orderly revolution (probably a contradiction in terms) and Marat as a champion of revolution at no matter what cost (probably no less a contradiction in terms since the law of diminishing returns seems to apply to revolutions as well as to the marketplace).

One final confession: If I were rewriting this book now I would hesitate to admit "to being partial to the materialistic interpretation of history" (p. xi). That change of view is not attributable to any devaluation in my mind of the importance of impersonal materialistic forces in the course of human events or of economic motives in the behavior of human beings but rather to an increasing conviction that the indeterminables (perhaps indescribables) which for want of a better name we call *chance* and *choice* or *free will* play roles—sometimes large, sometimes small, but rarely negligible—in historical and particularly in biographical developments. That change of view comes not so much because I trust the materialistic interpretation of history less as because I puzzle over the imponderables in individual behavior more. If that be treason, my Russian critics (who have sometimes mentioned me as one of the less objectionable among "bourgeois historians") will doubtless make the most of it.

Louis Gottschalk

Chicago
January 1967

PREFACE

If an apology is needed for this book, it is to be found in the words of the late Professor R. C. H. Catterall:

> All present lives of Marat are well-nigh valueless.
> The biography of Marat remains to be written.[1]

Professor Catterall had himself intended to write such a biography, but his premature death prevented his doing so. With that end in view, however, he added to the splendid collection of the numbers of Marat's journals already contained in the White Historical Library of Cornell University several other writings by Marat and most of the important works about him. The present author has been able to use not only this collection of Maratana, but also a few notes put at his disposal through the kindness of Mrs. Catterall.

The finest collection of material for the study of the career of Marat is, however, to be found at the British Museum Library. Among other valuable sources, the British Museum possesses the vast accumulation of notes and volumes that François Chevremont was able to gather in the course of a lifetime devoted to compiling a bibliography of Maratana and rehabilitating the damaged reputation of his subject. The Bibliothèque Nationale in Paris also is wealthy in Maratana —particularly in pamphlet literature. A few important documents are preserved in the Archives Nationale, and in the New York Public Library there is as complete a file of his journals as is to be found anywhere. While it may safely be assumed that somewhere there still is valuable material waiting to be discovered and published, a reasonably definite

[1] *American Historical Review*, XVI, 1910–1911, p. 35.

biography of Marat can even now be written from the available sources.

This book was not begun as a biography, however. It was originally a study of the development of the political theories of Marat. No careful exposition of that phase of Marat's life has yet appeared, and it was in order to fill that lacuna that the present work was undertaken. More recently, sufficient details regarding the other phases of Marat's political career have been added to justify the title of this book. Nevertheless, the chief emphasis is still upon his political philosophy. The reader will not find here the trivialities of Marat's amours, adventures, and family life. Nor will he find all of the familiar hair-raising tales about the Friend of the People. Occasionally the author has narrated such anecdotes where he has believed them to be true. But when he has had good reason to consider them false, he has sometimes refuted them, but more often has preferred to neglect them entirely as unworthy of serious attention.

The author has likewise tried to avoid the facile explanation of Marat's vagaries by pigeon-holing him as insane, anarchistic, or bloodthirsty. Marat was a human being—an extraordinary one, to be sure, but one whose conduct can be accounted for without insisting upon abnormalities, or without recourse (to use the words of a recent hysterical writer on him) to "the region of the supernatural," to "a belief in demoniacal possession." At the same time, a conscious attempt has been made to avoid the tendency of the biographer to idealize his subject. Marat's weak as well as his strong points have been treated *nullo discrimine* and without undue emphasis. If the reader finds, upon perusal of the following pages, that he cannot decide whether to admire or despise Marat, the author will feel that his task has been well accomplished. It has recently become a fad among biographers to rehabilitate damaged souls and to damage rehabilitated or entirely immaculate souls. The present writer has tried to do neither. He has not endeavored to depict either a hero or a villain, but to reproduce, as far as he has been able, a historical character who once thought, acted, and exerted his influence as circumstances permitted.

The biographer, knowing just what his subject will do next, is sometimes in a position to explain thoughts, decisions, and actions more ably and accurately than could the subject himself or any of his contemporaries. The danger is that it is very easy to assume that because something did happen, the causes of it are to be found in what we know to have gone before, whereas the true reasons may be entirely unknown. *Post hoc* is not necessarily *propter hoc* any more in the case of a single individual than in the development of events involving societies and nations. The assumption of *post hoc ergo propter hoc* has been a pitfall that the present biographer has assiduously tried to avoid, though it has gaped before him frequently, because he has taken special pains to tell not only what the events of Marat's life were, but also why they occurred.

The impulse to use the jargon of modern psychologists has also been very great. So many superior people have been found of late to have had an inferiority complex that one is sorely tempted to attribute the vagaries of Marat to the same weakness. But the author, a mere historian, has at no time mastered the science of psychology and has therefore not dared to attempt a psychoanalysis of Marat. He has had to be content simply with an old-fashioned "character study." If he has used the terminology of the Freudians at all, it has been only for the sake of convenience and with no intention of interpreting Marat in a pseudo-Freudian manner. The author has likewise had occasion to regret that he is not a specialist in omniscience when he has had to discuss Marat's activity in physics and medicine. To evaluate Marat's work in both these fields, he has been obliged to depend upon the judgment of others.

Furthermore, the author confesses to being partial to the materialistic interpretation of history. If material motives have been neglected to a considerable extent in this study, it was not because of preference, but because not enough evidence was available to enable a conscientious historian to assign as motives what for lack of such evidence rested solely upon strong presumptive grounds. This difficulty is enhanced by the fact that the accuracy of Marat, who is naturally our chief source of information, is not always to be trusted. For political and other purposes, he exaggerated the truth grossly. Very seldom were his narrations of events entirely fictitious, but it is no small task to extract the kernel of truth from many of his statements. Regarding his political theories, of course, his own works must be the principal and often the only source, and in this respect, while his sincerity may be questioned, they have to be relied upon for their purport.

Because of the many moot points in Marat's career, there will be many differences of opinion and even some quarreling about facts. For that reason an attempt has been made to furnish a complete bibliography. In order not to make it unnecessarily large, however, references to works that have not actually proved valuable in this study have been omitted. Footnotes have been used only where they have been deemed essential, as, for example, when facts were comparatively unknown or in dispute.

In conclusion, the author wishes to record his indebtedness to Laura Riding Gottschalk, whose time and efforts have been devoted to this book to a degree second only to his own; to his colleague Mr. Hill Shine, who has examined the manuscript and rendered other valuable assistance; to President George Colvin, Misses Sara Landau and Margaret Kirwan, Professors R. S. Cotterill and Rolf Johannesen for help in reading

PREFACE

proof or other substantial aid; to Miss Augusta Schoening for assistance in preparing the index; and to Professor Carl Becker, to whose guidance and inspiration this work is largely due and to whom it is therefore fittingly dedicated.

Louisville, Kentucky   L. R. G.
1927

TABLE OF CONTENTS

It is difficult to describe a personality. Every man is a riddle, not for others alone, but for himself likewise. It is presumptuous to claim a knowledge of one who is not known even by himself. Yet we cannot help passing judgments on character, for to do so is a necessary part of life. Not one of those we believe ourselves to know, not one of our friends, not one of those we love, is as we see him. In many cases he is utterly different from our picture. We wander amid the phantoms we create. Yet we have to judge; we have to act.

ROMAIN ROLLAND

CHAPTER I

EARLY LIFE, CHARACTER, AND IDEAS

OUR modern age is one in which the task of manufacturing an article of commerce is carefully divided into many minute and distinct operations. This—a result of the revolution in industry that has been going on since the eighteenth century—has also had its effect upon the professions. Our doctors are learned only in medicine, and the best ones in but a small branch of that art; our lawyers seldom consider themselves authorities on all phases of the law; and our teachers are experts either in philosophy or physics or Spanish literature or any of a host of other subjects, but rarely in any two of these. Not only must shoes go through many hands before they are ready to be worn, but an invalid must run the gauntlet of dentist, optician, chiropodist, physician, etc.; any but the least important cases at law receives the attention of a corps of clerks and attorneys; and the student, once the ward of half-a-dozen pedagogues, now is exposed to the learning of half-a-hundred or more. Ours is the age of specialization.

This was not true before the Industrial Revolution made necessary our elaborate division of labor in industry. In the early eighteenth century the man of means and culture dabbled in many branches of knowledge. Montesquieu, best known to the world as a political philosopher, also wrote poetry, drama, history, and physiology; Voltaire was all but a universal genius; Goethe in Germany, Priestley in England, and Franklin in America were equally versatile. Yet the entire era was tending toward a political climax. Whatever a man's

vocation might have been, political interests probably monopolized a large part of his leisure, if he was at all awake
to the problems of his time.   Therefore, when the long-
heralded French Revolution came, it was natural that prominent men should devote their principal attention to political
events.   When a man has several varying interests, it is
not so difficult for him to emphasize one of these in case of
emergency as it would be to change altogether a career bound
up in a single highly specialized field.   And so, without any
very great sacrifice and probably without realizing that such a
step would change the course of their lives, Bailly the astrono-
mer, Condorcet the philosopher, Lafayette the soldier, Talley-
rand the priest—all became primarily statesmen and par-
liamentarians, abandoning their professions entirely or giving
them but scanty notice thereafter.

Among those thus affected by the French Revolution was
Jean Paul Marat.   Born in Boudry, Neuchâtel, on May 24,
1743, before the century had half run its course, and dying on
July 13, 1793, when it had reached its culmination, he re-
flects admirably the catholicity of interests so prevalent
among his contemporaries.   He was trained for a career in
medicine, but before the Revolution came to require all of his
energies, he had written, in addition to a few medical tracts,
two novels, one volume on criminology, several scientific
works on fire, electricity, and light, two treatises on meta-
physics, a panegyric of Montesquieu, and an historical inquiry
into the nature and growth of despotism.   The events of 1789
and the years that followed cut short a career that bade fair
to become famous in the scientific world and gave us a Marat
known chiefly as a man of politics, a leading figure in that
crowded era which, after all, occupied but four years of a
lifetime that extended over half a century.

It was into a lower middle-class home that Marat was born,
the oldest of six children.   His father (who spelled his name

Mara) was a Sardinian Catholic who later turned Calvinist. He has been variously described as a monk, a doctor, a teacher of languages, and a designer of figures on cloth, but contemporary documents mention only the last two professions. The story goes that he had run away from a Sardinian abbey, preferring the freedom of the world to the restrictions of a monastic life, and had eventually found himself in Switzerland. There he married Louise Cabrol, a Genevan Calvinist, who became by him the mother of six children. The first of these was Jean Paul Mara, who later, in order to appear more French, changed his name to Marat. One of his brothers was to achieve a reputation as a tutor in the court of Catherine the Great of Russia under the name of Monsieur de Boudry, and a sister, Albertine, after having had nothing to do with her oldest brother for the greater part of his life, was to become the subject of numerous encomiums because of the faithfulness with which she devoted her last years to sanctifying his memory.

The family seems to have lived in moderate circumstances as long as Jean Paul was with them, but, nevertheless, he tells us, he received "a very careful education in his paternal home." Until he emerges, about 1765, from a state of almost complete oblivion and takes up his abode in England, we know very little about him. Fain would we believe him when he tells us that he was a high-spirited child who, having refused to go back to school when his teacher had humiliated him, had jumped out of a window when he was locked up in his room for punishment. This misadventure, he claimed, left a permanent scar upon his forehead. Fain also would we believe that he was a precocious and ambitious youth when he tells us that at the age of five he wanted to become a school teacher, at fifteen a university professor, at eighteen an author, and at twenty a creative genius. But at forty-five or fifty, one is likely to look back upon one's childhood and youth with a tender warmth that renders it difficult to tell only the truth.   All that we can say with certainty is that Marat seems to have left his home when sixteen years of age, to have acted as tutor to the child of Paul Nairac, a wealthy sugar refiner of Bordeaux, later a deputy to the National Assembly, to have studied medicine at the University of Bordeaux, and to have left after two years to continue his studies at Paris.   In 1760 he appears to have petitioned King Louis XV for permission to accompany the Abbé Chappe d'Auteroche to Tobolsk in order to observe the passage of Venus over the sun.   The request, however, received no attention.   In short, before Marat's career may be said to have begun, his story resembles that of many a son of poor parents who has secured his education by dint of hard work and self-support.   There is some evidence that before he finally settled in England, he had already lived in London for a short time and had also made brief visits to Dublin, Edinburgh, the Hague, Utrecht, and Amsterdam.   He was now (1765) twenty-two years of age.

His career during his first years in England is obscure. When he comes into clearer view, we find him no longer a self-supporting student, but a member of the best society, enjoying an extensive medical practice and a considerable reputation as a writer.   He resided in Soho, at that time the aristocratic quarter of London, and counted among his friends Lord Lyttleton and the famous artist Angelica Kauffman. In 1775, on the recommendation of Doctors Hugh James and William Buchan, two contemporary physicians of note, he received the honorary degree of Doctor of Medicine from St. Andrews University of Scotland.   How much credit for this honor is due to Marat's accomplishments it is difficult to say, for it will be remembered that St. Andrews is the university of which Dr. Johnson, because of its notorious practice of selling its degrees, said that it would grow richer by degrees. It is interesting to note that the diploma granted the degree to *Sieur Mara*, and that a *t* was added afterward by the Sieur himself.

During his sojourn in England Marat published an *Essay on the Human Soul*, which was followed by a larger treatise entitled *A Philosophical Essay on Man*. *The Monthly Review* (1772, XLVI, p. 254) justly considered the *Essay on the Human Soul* puerile, although "displaying talents which admit of cultivation and improvement." It was more favorably impressed with the *Essay on Man*, of which Lord Lyttleton and Professor Collingnon of Cambridge University also spoke highly. In both of these essays (the *Essay on the Human Soul* was reprinted as a chapter in the *Essay on Man*) the author accepted the duality of body and soul and attempted to analyze their reciprocal influence upon each other. He met then and has met since with bitter ridicule because he contended that the seat of the soul is in the meninges.

But convinced that all adverse criticism was dictated either by ignorance or malice, he undertook to propagate his theories upon the continent. The *Essay on Man* was translated into French and published in three volumes at Amsterdam (1775–1776). It did not receive as favorable a reception in France as it had in England, where the materialism of Holbach and Helvétius, whom it attacked, was less fashionable than across the Channel. Marat had wished to have the whole of the French edition of the *Essay on Man* shipped from Amsterdam to Paris for sale. The shipment, however, was delayed by the customs officials for some time, and Marat finally decided that it was being held up by the intrigues of rival scientists who desired to prevent the spread of his ideas. By threats and persistence he eventually obtained the release of his books, but only, he claimed, after some of them had been scattered in countries outside of France. Such, at least, is Marat's own story, but from what will shortly be explained of his character, it is quite likely that he was mistaken, that there was some reason for the delay other than that of jealous scheming. Marat very easily convinced himself, when things went wrong, that he was being unjustly persecuted and martyred by the enemies of his cause.

In England, in the meantime, he continued to foster his reputation. In 1774, on the occasion of an election of Parliament, hoping to awaken the citizens of England to a sense of their civic duty, he wrote *The Chains of Slavery*, of which we shall hear more presently. This work, he asserted with what may or may not be truth, won for him the assiduous persecution of governmental authorities, the lively approbation of patriotic societies, and membership in several political clubs. He rounded out his literary activity in England by publishing two tracts in the field of medicine—one on the cure of gleets and the other on a certain disease of the eye. These were republished in 1891 by Bailey, the librarian of the Royal College of Surgeons of England. Marat also received the distinction of an award of citizenship in Newcastle, where he seems to have lived for a time, for services that he rendered during an epidemic.

These facts are enough to show that the stories of the life of obscurity and even of crime that Marat led in England are merely the inventions of his enemies or the romantic legends that very often spring up, no one knows how, about the unusual characters of history. He is supposed by some to have earned his living in Edinburgh by teaching tambouring—a curious occupation indeed for one who had studied medicine. Others believe that he taught school at Warrington Academy—for which, to be sure, his tutoring at Bordeaux would have been some preparation and which, if there were any supporting evidence other than two letters alleged to have been (but prob-

ably not) [1] written by him asking for the hand of the daugh-
ter of the principal of the Academy, it would not be impossible
to believe.   It has even been maintained that in 1786–1787,
at a time when we know he was engrossed in scientific work in
Paris, he was in Bristol selling books and serving a term for
debt.   The servant of one Mr. Ireland, it seems, thought he
recognized in Marat, whom he saw in France in 1792, a man
whom his master had befriended in the Bristol jail, and informed Mr. Ireland of his impression.   Mr. Ireland told a
friend of his, a Mr. Harford, who as a student at Warrington
Academy had or thought he had had an instructor in foreign
languages named Le Maitre *alias* Mara, whom he had afterwards seen at the hulks at Woolwich serving a term for having robbed the Ashmolean Museum.   Others had already
tried to make of this Le Maitre *alias* Mara the Marat who was
then creating such a commotion in France, as well as to con-
nect the French radical Marat with a certain White, who was
said to have called his children Marat and who had conducted
a tambouring establishment in Edinburgh.   What could have
been more natural than for Mr. Ireland's friend, Mr. Harford,
to assume that this Marat, whom Mr. Ireland knew to have
served a term in Bristol, was the same man whom he had seen
in Woolwich?   What more natural, then, than for Dr.
Turner, a schoolmate of Mr. Harford's, in writing a history
of Warrington Academy, to inform us that "there is great reason to believe" that Le Maitre *alias* Mara, who had taught
French at the Academy in 1772, who had robbed the Ashmolean Museum in 1776, who had been sentenced to Woolwich
in 1777, and who later, having failed as a bookseller, had
served another sentence in jail in Bristol, was the great figure
of the French Revolution?   Learned authorities have ever
since debated whether this was the real history of Marat's life

[1] See *The Criminality of Marat* in *The South Atlantic Quarterly* for April
1926, pp. 156–157.

in England, and all because the servant of a Bristol philanthropist thought he saw in Marat making a speech to the Convention in 1792 a prisoner for debt whom his master had befriended half a dozen years before, and because some of the aliases sported by a gentleman or, more probably, several gentlemen of criminal proclivities in England, sounded like Marat. If all of this criminal activity must be associated with one man by that name, the facts would seem to fit Marat's brother John Peter much better than Marat himself, and would, incidentally, explain the resemblance of the Conventional and the inmate of the debtor's prison. But probably John Peter was no more guilty than Jean Paul. One Reverend G. Huddesford, author of some verses published in 1793 under the title of *Topsy Turvey*, has maintained that Marat served no less than nine terms in English jails—a statement which sounds extraordinary alongside of Marat's defiant declaration, made in 1790 in reply to the taunts of his enemies, that no one could find his name on the registers of the police of Bordeaux, where he had lived two years, London, where he had lived ten, The Hague, Utrecht, or Amsterdam, where he had lived one, Paris, where he had lived nineteen, or any other place in Europe that he had visited. As a matter of fact, Marat was neither poverty-stricken nor criminal while he lived in England. Quite the contrary is true: he was a person of some prominence and social position when in 1777 he returned from England to France.

Why he returned to France we do not know, unless we accept the untenable theory that as the robber Le Maitre he had escaped from the Woolwich Hulks and therefore considered the atmosphere of France more wholesome for the time being than that of England. The more probable explanation is that he was lured back to Paris by the prospects of a good position. At any rate, in the year of his arrival in France he became the doctor of the body-guard of the Count of Artois, an office

which he held for six years.   Carlyle and other unfriendly
historians would have us believe that, because the place of his
location during that interval was in a quarter known as the
Ecuries, Marat's position was that of a veterinary.   But a
glance at the *Almanac Royal* would have convinced them of
their error.   There he is listed as Doctor of the Body-Guard of
the Count of Artois until the appointment of his successor in
1786, although he resigned in 1783.   Awarded this position
because of his experience and reputation as a physician, he continued, while he held it, to increase his prestige, charging ex-
orbitant fees and boasting a wealthy clientele.   One of his
patients, the Marquise de Laubespine, had been given up by
all other doctors as hopelessly tubercular.   Yet Marat treated
her with such apparent success that she, together with others
who were familiar with the case and wrote about it to the
Gazette de Santé, believed that she had been entirely cured.
To a modern sceptic it would appear that most likely the
Marquise suffered from a disease quite other than tubercu-
losis, but the Marquise was convinced.   Brissot, whose memoirs, along with some letters of the Marquis de Laubespine,
are our chief source of information regarding this extraordinary cure, tells us that since the Marquis was an old rake, his
wife fell an easy victim to the charms of her remarkable
doctor and that their relations for some time were very inti-
mate.   Marat himself, in a recently published letter, speaks
of her as a good friend.   There would have been very few in
the gallant eighteenth century who would have cared to inquire further than that into the relationship of the Doctor and
his patient; and beyond that we of a more Victorian age
cannot inquire.

The Marquise's cure had been effected by means of an *eau-
factice-antipulmonique*, which Marat's increasing reputation
enabled him to float on the market.   In 1778 this remedy was
analyzed by Abbé Teissier, doctor-regent of the Faculty of

Medicine of the Royal Medical Society, and found to be little more than chalk and water. This sale of patent medicines was an offense out of which his future enemies were to make much political capital, but for the present, if we are to believe Marat's own testimony about himself, he became known as the "doctor of the incurables." There is extant a letter from him to one of his patients, who nevertheless died under his care, referring to him by that high-sounding title. Whether it was deserved or not, his success not only as a lung specialist, but also as an eye doctor, brought him numerous patients from wealthy and noble families.

In the period between his resignation from the retinue of the Count of Artois and the outbreak of the Revolution (1783–1789), he appears to have devoted himself almost entirely to scientific investigation. Altogether, from 1777 until 1789, he published eight books of physical research on fire, electricity, light, and optics, in addition to other less important works. These publications earned distinction for him abroad as well as in France. One of them—*Mémoire sur l'Électricité médicale*—was crowned by the Royal Academy of Rouen on August 6, 1783. Marat had already touched upon the medical properties of electricity in his *Recherches physiques sur l'électricité*. He seems to have been instrumental in persuading the Academy at Rouen to propose that question for a contest. While approving his essay, the Academy had felt called upon to express its regret "that the author had not put more amenity into his terms" in refuting the opinion of the Abbé Berthelon, one of the predecessors of Marat in this field of research. Characteristically enough, Marat declared in his introduction to the volume that he had re-read his manuscript with this comment in mind and could find nothing in it that a self-respecting author ought to have hesitated to say. He concluded that it was simply as a consolation to the Abbé, one of the members of the Academy, that this criticism of his work had been made.

Three other books—*Recherches physiques sur le feu, Découvertes sur la lumière,* and *Recherches physiques sur l'électricité,* all written between 1780 and 1782, while he was still with the Count of Artois—in which he emphasizes his theory that fire and electricity are derived respectively from igneous and electrical fluids, were translated into German and published at Leipsic by Professor Weigel in 1782–1784. In 1788 appeared the *Mémoires académiques ou nouvelles découvertes sur la lumière,* which contained, along with four other essays, a brief *Mémoire sur les vrais causes des couleurs que presentent les lames de verre, les bulles de savon, et autres matières diaphanes extrèmement minces,* which on August 2, 1786 had become the second of Marat's works to have been honored by the Academy of Rouen. This essay carried off the prize in a contest held by the Academy. The reputation of Marat as a scientist grew. *The Journal de Paris* (April 6, 1780) contained an advertisement to the effect that a certain M. Felissier, a member of several academies, would give a course of demonstrations and lectures upon the theories laid down by Marat; and we know from other sources that this course was quite well attended by an appreciative audience. Benjamin Franklin was present at a demonstration of Marat's experiments, and seemed favorably impressed, although he does not appear to have given as much attention as Marat solicited and afterwards claimed to have received from him. Goethe in his own work on *Farbenlehre* considered Marat's results obtained *mit viel Scharfsinn und Beobachtungsgabe.* Sage, Lamarck, Cousin, Condorcet, and Leroy regarded his investigations with favor, and a few scientists of more recent times have expressed their appreciation of his efforts.

Besides his scientific volumes, Marat had also published

(1780) a *Plan de législation criminelle*, which Brissot later included in his *Bibliothèque philosophique du législateur, etc.*, although many years after, when his attitude toward Marat had completely changed, he asserted that he had done so against his better judgment. In addition, there were three works which Marat wrote before 1789, although they were not published until long after his death. These were *Les Aventures de jeune Comte Patowski* (edited in 1848 as *Un Roman du coeur*), *Les Lettres polonaises,* and an *Eloge de Montesquieu.* The first two, probably written in the early seventies, were novels somewhat after the style of Rousseau's *Nouvelle Héloïse,* [1] and the last was an enthusiastic appreciation of the author of *L'Esprit des lois.* This was submitted in one of the many prize competitions held at this time by the numerous academies, as were some of the other works already considered. It failed, like most of the others, to win any honors, and remained to be unearthed decades later and published for its historical rather than its literary value.

If, as Marat confessed, it was his ambition at eighteen to become a novelist, it is not difficult, even for one who is not a keen critic of literature, to understand why, upon failing to find publishers for his two novels, he decided in his thirties to seek another career. Everybody of any literary pretentions has at one time or another essayed a novel like the *Adventures of the Young Count Patowski.* It is the romance of a Polish noble who, separated from his fiancée by a civil war in which their respective families take opposing sides, after many

---

[1] The authenticity of the *Lettres polonaises* has been questioned (Chevremont, *Index du Bibliophile,* etc., p. 238). See, however, *Polish Letters,* published by the Bibliophile Society, translated from the original manuscript in the possession of Mr. Bixby, vol. I, pp. 79 ff. A comparison of the facsimiles of chirography, also contained therein, is sufficient to show that the writing of the manuscript is in Marat's hand. The date of composition is easily fixed between 1772 and 1777, for evidently it was written in England, which Marat left in 1777, and contains a reference to the Partition of Poland (II, 196), which gives us our date *non ante quem.*

melodramatic incidents finally succeeds in winning her.   The author is deeply agitated over the sorry disruption of Poland, but no hint of the future revolutionary can be obtained from the glamour which he weaves about the noble figures of his story.   The *Polish Letters* is a better piece of writing.   It is the story of a Polish Prince, Kamia, who, like Rica and Usbek of Montesquieu's *Persian Letters*, narrates at length for the delectation of his friends back home his experiences in France, Holland, Switzerland, and England—the lands with which Marat was most familiar.   Since Kamia is not as profound or as interesting as Rica, the *Polish Letters* are dull in comparison with Montesquieu's work.   But they are an important key to the development of their author's *Weltanschauung*, and we shall meet Kamia again when we come to discuss his creator's political philosophy.

Much has been written by biographers unfriendly to Marat to show that he was a charlatan in both medicine and science. There is a story to the effect that he once attempted to bewilder the contemporary scientist Charles by proving that resin would conduct electricity, using a piece of resin in which he had hidden a needle for his demonstration.   This, the story continues, resulted in a duel in which Marat was worsted. That a duel was planned between Charles and Marat we have sufficient evidence to believe.   The cause for the umbrage between the two, however, was this.   Charles had spoken disparagingly of Marat in a public lecture.   Marat called upon him at his home for an explanation and there arose a dispute which resulted in the exchange of blows, each claiming the other to have been the initial aggressor.   There were no struggles between Charles and Marat at the former's lectures, as some legends have it, although it is not at all improbable that Marat might have attended one or more of them.   After their fisticuffs at Charles' home, a duel actually was arranged, but through the interference of the police, it

never took place.   Thus the needle-and-resin story is shown
to have as little foundation as some of the other tales to which
Michelet, Carlyle, and, more recently, Phipson have given
credence.   On the whole, there can be little doubt that Marat's
work as a scientist entitles him to be considered something
more than a charlatan and quack.

Such was Marat's career before 1789.   It was not one which
was calculated to make a heretic and radical of him.   Coming from a lower middle-class family and having led what was
probably an ordinary student life, he finally earned a reputation and a comfortable income among the wealthy bourgeoisie in both England and France.   One might expect that
his ideas at this time, influenced by the milieu in which he
found himself, would be entirely conventional, conforming to
the dilettanteism of the eighteenth century salon.   And so they
were.   Monarchy seemed to him to be the best form of government for a country as large as France, and he considered
a good monarch "the noblest work of the Creator, the most
fit to honor human nature and to represent the divine."   His
book on *The Chains of Slavery* was an acrimonious attack
upon despots, but not a word was breathed therein against good
monarchs.   Such, to be sure, he felt were rare; yet in his
letters we find that he believed that Spain had "a great king,"
"a good king" in the person of Charles III, and that Frederick
of Prussia was "the greatest of kings."   But then much of
his confidence in these two representatives of royal excellence
may be attributed to the fact that at the time that he wrote
these words of praise he was hoping for favors from them.

Nor was Marat's king a figurehead; he was the chief minister of the law, a magistrate with a definite duty to perform
and for which he was to be held accountable.   Although Marat
advocated general religious tolerance, he believed it best that
there should be but one religious sect in a state and that that
should be linked with the political organization.   True to

his conservative background, he declared that the government itself ought to be managed by the wealthy, by those who had "the largest stake in the public weal." For the common people, on the whole, were ignorant, did not know their rights, and hardly perceived that there was anything wrong with the world. They were satisfied; "the disorder which reigns at present upon the earth disturbs very few except the philosophers."

This remark comes from the *Polish Letters*, a novel which appears to have been the result of much anxious introspection. In it an Englishman whom the author designates as the Sage pointed out the practical difficulties in the way of reforming society and maintained that it is necessary to leave things very much as they are.   The Sage's concluding observation was:

> Great volumes have been written on the duties of man; I find them no less vain than ridiculous. All my morality is included in this maxim: Be obedient to the laws of your country.

With such a Socratic philosophy, Marat might without any hesitation accept employment from a prince of the blood and act not only as one of his medical staff but also as a sort of confidant, writing letters in order to defend his employer from verbal attack. Nor is it surprising, considering the passion of the period for titles (that "born republican" Madame Roland sought tirelessly to have her husband ennobled, and Danton for a time was D'Anton), to discover Marat petitioning for a patent of nobility and using a coat of arms.   From these various acts and opinions the inference may be drawn that the pre-Revolutionary Marat was a complacent, conservative spirit, endowed with a goodly share of middle-class virtues.

The seeds of discontent, however, had already been sown. Marat was an omnivorous reader and consequently was exposed to all the new philosophical ideas which floated around in the intellectual atmosphere of his century. The preface to his *Essay on Man* shows that he had studied, in preparation for it, the works of the physiologists and philosophers of all ages from Hippocrates to Helvétius. The books cited in the footnotes of the *Chains of Slavery* number over seventy, culled from the historical classics of Greece, Rome, Spain, Italy, England, and France.

But it was not from the classics of any nation that he harvested his crop of ideas. This was the Age of Enlightenment. Newton had already shown that the physical relations of the Universe were governed by ascertainable laws of nature, and Locke had contended that human understanding was a product of nature. Adding Newton and Locke together, the eighteenth century argued that human relations must likewise be governed by ascertainable laws of nature. By an exertion of the reason, then, it was possible to discover how to regulate the affairs of mankind. Certainly there could be little worse than the way in which they were already regulated. And so Montesquieu wrote his *Spirit of the Laws* to urge that governments ought to conform to natural environment. Voltaire penned histories and pamphlets against an unnatural, intolerant religion. Rousseau idealized the state of nature and the social compact that was the natural source of governmental authority, and gave *Émile* a natural education. Other lesser writers engaged in feverish literary activity to shed the purging light of reason upon the unnatural abuses of an age which they could not fail to realize was an Ancient Regime.

Inevitably Marat came under the influence of many of the great writers of his own era—Montesquieu, Rousseau, Voltaire, Beccaria, Diderot, D'Alembert, and Raynal. It was the first two of these to whom he was the most indebted. Voltaire had earned his everlasting hatred by reviewing the French version of his *Essay on Man* with scathing criticism.

This was perhaps in revenge for Marat's having referred to him as "the inconsequent Voltaire" and having spoken of his friend Helvétius disparagingly.   Diderot had likewise mentioned this work unfavorably.   He had said plainly, "Marat does not know what he is talking about when he speaks of the action of the soul upon the body."   But Marat's antagonism to him and his famous collaborator D'Alembert was due rather to their unfriendly attitude toward Rousseau than to any personal displeasure.   As for Raynal, it is Lamartine who is responsible for the statement that Marat was chiefly under his intellectual sway.   To be sure, Marat did once speak of Raynal in a highly laudatory vein (*Ami du Peuple*, no. 195, August 18, 1790, pp. 4–5).   But Lamartine also names the Bible as one of the books which especially influenced Marat, and there is as little reason for singling out the one as the other.   Lamartine, in this case as in others, has allowed his poetic imagination to run away with his historical judgment.   There is more cause to consider the influence of Beccaria.   Though the great Italian criminologist received but scanty mention in the voluminous writings of Marat, the latter's *Plan de législation criminelle* resembled the former's *Traité des délits et des peines* to such an extent as to have led to the accusation of plagiarism by later writers— a charge which was nevertheless not justified.

But another and perhaps greater source of inspiration and knowledge for this work must certainly have been Montesquieu's *Esprit des lois*.   Marat spoke of Montesquieu as "the greatest man whom the century had produced," greater even than Rousseau, since Rousseau owned no property, had no family, and therefore ran smaller risks in attacking society. In his *Éloge de Montesquieu*, Marat, although he never accepted Montesquieu's whole-hearted appreciation of the English constitution, indited an ardent panegyric of the author of *The Spirit of the Laws* (perhaps with an eye to winning the prize for which the essay was submitted). In later years, Marat declared that Montesquieu, had he lived, would have been the only one fit to educate the Dauphin correctly as the future ruler of France—a statement that would appear to overlook the claims of the author of *Émile*.

Yet, if Marat held Montesquieu the greatest of all philosophers, Rousseau was to his mind "the greatest man whom the century would have produced if Montesquieu had not existed." The second volume of the French edition of the *Essay on Man* ends with an invocation to Jean Jacques. Mallet du Pan claimed to have witnessed Marat reading to street-corner audiences from the *Contrat Social* even as early as 1788. There is no way of verifying the truth of this allegation, but even if untrue, it at least illustrates the influence which contemporaries believed Rousseau to have had upon Marat. Michelet, a later but perhaps even more unfriendly critic, called Marat "the ape of Rousseau." The fact is that, even though Marat himself did not realize it, Rousseau's *Social Contract* and *Discourse on the Origins of Inequality* were apparently the sources of more of his ideas than any of the products of Montesquieu's pen.

The reading of such literature had much the same effect upon the conservative Marat as the reading of the most brilliant modern radical writers might well have upon any professional man of equal intelligence in our own day. Marat's spirit was profoundly agitated. This can be seen from his *Polish Letters*, which was very evidently autobiographical. It is the story of a young Polish prince who traveled in the same countries as Marat had visited. In the course of his journeys, he meets first a hermit, who torments his soul with unconventional and disturbingly radical notions, and then a sage, who calms his troubled mind and brings him back into harmony with the world. The conflicting philosophies of the hermit and the sage were but a reflection of the struggle going on in Marat's soul; and though the story ends with a feeling of God's-in-his-Heaven-all's-right-with-the-world, Marat's own mental strife left him less peaceful and composed. After the composition of the *Polish Letters*, the Marat who had written *Les Aventures de jeune Comte Patowski*, an adolescent novel that wrapped nobles and nobility in a veil of romantic glory, now became the Marat who penned passionate diatribes against despotism and barbaric criminal codes.

An examination of these diatribes, too, will reveal that though they were on the whole conservative, they contained occasional passages which indicated that the radical Friend of the People of the future was in the process of development. *The Chains of Slavery* is a study of the means employed by princes to make themselves constantly more powerful and despotic. The development of despotism everywhere and always is attributed by the author to a deliberate and conscious effort on the part of rulers, who conspire with one another, with the clergy, with the legislature, and with the ministry to hoodwink the people and to keep them in subjection. By showing how this vast conspiracy had succeeded throughout the ages Marat hoped to rouse the British electorate to the necessity of exerting greater care in the choice of representatives in the general elections of 1774. There was really little in the book to cause Lord North to pursue its author with the malignant persistency with which Marat claimed to have been persecuted, unless it was a rather astute criticism of the English constitution as it then existed. Nor was there any great merit in it which should have impelled the liberal societies of England to honor him as much as he alleged he was honored by them, unless it was its absolute frankness and daring in attacking the evils which he had occasion to mention. On the whole, therefore, Marat's elaborate account of the circumstances surrounding the publication of the *Chains of*

Slavery—written as it was, almost a score of years after the event, in the French edition of 1793, when the memory of the actual occurrences was dim, and intended as it was to win for him the support and admiration of the French readers— was a gross exaggeration of perhaps one or two facts of little importance. It is true, for example, that he did at this time leave England for Holland, and perhaps because he himself at least suspected that the North Government was persecuting him. It is likewise true that he received (July 15, 1774) a diploma of membership in the Grand Lodge of Freemasons of London (which, nineteen years later, he could without great difficulty glorify into three letters of affiliation from liberal societies sent in a golden box); and this honor may have been conferred upon him because of the merit of his book in the eyes of the liberal organizations of England. Furthermore, since we know that even in his last years, when he was weakened by disease and by the persecutions of his enemies, he was capable of the most extraordinary labor, his story that he finished his manuscript of the *Chains of Slavery* only after working twenty-one hours daily for three months and consuming enormous quantities of black coffee, and that after his labors he fell into a state of coma from which he was roused only by the powers of music and rest, does not sound so utterly fantastic. But there is little else to support his almost preposterous claims of bitter oppression on the one hand and enthusiastic support on the other.

The work itself, however, is one of the most important sources of knowledge we have of the political theories of Marat before the French Revolution. Having lived in England longer than Montesquieu, Marat was more aware of the defects of the English constitution. He perceived the vices of the rotten-borough system, feared the power which the king exerted over Parliament through bribery and the right to create peers, and was indignant at the limitations upon

the right of suffrage and the property qualifications required
of members of Parliament.   In short, he urged a program of
reform which the Chartists of the following century were
destined to adopt.   Yet, just as the Prince of the *Lettres
polonaises* had found England "perhaps the only country in
the world that a wise man would choose as an asylum," so
in the *Chains of Slavery* Marat still believed the constitution
of England to be "a monument of political wisdom if compared to others."   As a whole, then, the volume was of the
type that almost any Chathamite in England might have written at the time.   Marat's attitude at this juncture was that
of the reserved liberal, not that of the extreme radical.

There are in the *Chains of Slavery*, however, a few intimations of the more extraordinary views that were to dominate the author's later life.   The arraignment of despotism
had led him to attack religion in general, and Christianity in
particular, because it countenanced despotism.   An occasion
was also presented for a disputation against capital punishment except in extreme cases.   But what is most important
in the education of the Marat of the Revolution is that the
writing of the book caused him to reflect seriously upon the
sovereignty of the people.   As a true disciple of Rousseau,
Marat used the term *sovereign* to designate the people at
large and repudiated it as a title for the monarch.   His
sovereign people act through representatives, but only because
such a procedure is more practical.   These representatives,
like Rousseau's, have no authority to enact any legislation
whatsoever without first obtaining the consent of their constituencies.   Thus it is assured that the people will be the
ruler of the nation and the king merely its leading magistrate.

As a logical consequence of his belief in the sovereignty
of the people came his sympathy for the poor and needy.   For
a doctor who, later at any rate, commonly charged as much
as thirty-six livres for a consultation, such an interest was,

to say the least, remarkable. Perhaps he remembered his own poor origin and his struggles as a student. At any rate, Marat had already in his *Polish Letters* commented upon the wretched condition of the poor. In that book the hermit, whose philosophy had made Prince Kamia feel so utterly wretched until he met the more agreeable sage, had preached a gospel of redistribution of wealth upon a basis of equality and had declaimed against the injustice of private property. This was three-quarters of a century before Proudhon dared to startle the world with his famous epigram: property is theft. In the *Chains of Slavery* this theme received less attention. That the feeling of its author for the down-trodden had nevertheless not abated is clear from his arraignment of mismanagement in poor-houses, hospitals, and prisons. And here, too, the injustice of certain laws weighing most heavily upon the unfortunate members of society was assailed.

It was left for a later publication of Marat's to renew the bitterness of the hermit's attack upon the prevailing social system. This was the *Plan de législation criminelle*, a study of crimes and their punishments, which Marat himself thought was "the least imperfect" of all the works that left his pen.[1] Here also is to be found the same deep respect for good princes, unfortunately few in number, that he had already evinced. Nevertheless, he once more affirmed his belief in the sovereignty of the people. With this as his premise, he argued, now as before, that the people and not the king form the nation, and that murder of the king is consequently simply assassination and not *lèse majesté*. Because Joseph II

---

[1] *Ami du Peuple*, no. 169, July 1790, p. 8. *The Plan de législation criminelle* was originally published in 1780, after having failed to win a prize for which it was submitted. That edition, however, is *"introuvable dans le commerce"* (Chevremont, *Index du Bibliophile*, p. 22). The edition of 1790 has been used here and collated with large extracts and comments contained in Gunther, *Marat als Criminalist*, in *Der Gerichtssaal*, 1902, vol. LXI, based upon the edition of the work in Brissot's *Bibliothèque philosophique du législateur, etc.*

of Austria shortly afterwards issued a decree to this effect for his realms, in subsequent editions of the *Plan de législation criminelle* Marat assured his readers that the influence of his volume on the rulers of Europe had been tremendous. The king, his argument continued, is merely the first minister of the law; he speaks only in its name and, should he exceed his legitimate power, may justly be resisted by his people.

This postulate led him to an examination of the extent to which a citizen ought to submit to the law; and in the course of his examination he found an opportunity for re-echoing the hermit's bitter denunciation of society.   He began by pointing out that property tended to accumulate in the hands of a few, leaving the many in hunger and poverty.   Since the lower classes really derive no advantages from society, he said, they can not be obliged to respect the laws of society.   Hence, if they gain by force the rights which are theirs by nature, any authority which opposes them is tyrannical.   If society must maintain the established order of things, it ought to provide food, shelter, and clothing for such unfortunates.   His insistence upon this point is emphatic:

> The right to possess is derived from that to live.   Therefore everything that is indispensable for our existence is ours, and nothing superfluous can belong to us legitimately as long as others lack necessities.   This is the legitimate foundation of all property, both in the state of society and in the state of nature.

He comes now to the logical conclusion of his thesis—the establishment of public workshops and a redistribution of ecclesiastical property which would leave sufficient in the hands of the clergy to enable them to live an edifying life, the remainder to be apportioned among the indigent in small lots.   Free public schools, to be maintained at the expense of the leisure class, also formed a part of his program.   If the worker, after having been given a fair opportunity to work and a salary proportionate to his labor, should nevertheless refuse to engage in a useful occupation, Marat claimed he ought then to be banished from the state.

Such a system of political and social reform, antedating the Chartists on the one hand and Louis Blanc on the other, would seem to label its champion a radical among radicals of his day. It must be remembered, however, that these utterances are gleaned from a multitude of others altogether commonplace. They are merely the specious arguments that any reader of Rousseau's *Discourse on Equality* and Montesquieu's *Spirit of the Laws*, seeking to win coronation by an academy for his work and to make a reputation for himself as a political philosopher, might very well have assimilated and revamped. Mably and Morelly, whom there is no reason to believe Marat had not studied, had also set them forth, and for fashionable society of the eighteenth century there was little in them that was novel or startling. While they serve to indicate where Marat's sympathies would lie in case of a future crisis, as yet they occupied but a small part of his thought and, despite the emphasis that the biographer must give them, took up little space in his writings. They reveal, however, the fact that Marat, like so many other people then and now, was a curious composite of conservatism and radicalism. This prosperous physician, devoted to his science, dabbling in other phases of knowledge, content with the monarchical system of government, and believing that only a few doctrinaires were troubled by the defects of society, nevertheless had been induced to advocate the theories of the most radical thinkers of his time. He was far from being a rabid reformer in those days, but he did have a very definite opinion about certain political and social abuses.

There was another factor that prevented the prosperous Doctor Jean Paul Marat from being entirely complacent. Recognized scientist though he was, he had failed to win the membership in the Academy of Sciences that he so much coveted. Although he had submitted a large part of his work for its approval, he pretended that the failure was a matter of indifference to him and that, had he but shown a willingness to secure the election, it would have been granted. Nevertheless, he felt the slight to his scientific attainments keenly, and it was one of the reasons why the Revolution, when it came, so easily changed the scientist into the politician.

To appreciate why this was so, it is necessary only to understand that the salient point of Marat's character was a morbid expectation of unjust treatment. Such apparent neglect of his work, whether intentional or not, gave rise in his mind to the dread that he was being persecuted intentionally and maliciously. This obsession, which he had already entertained on two separate occasions in England—once with regard to the publication of his *Chains of Slavery* and again in connection with delay in the delivery of the French edition of his *Essay on Man*—and which we shall find recurring time and again in his later career, came to him so frequently that some, with the biographer's anxiety to label all human emotions, have maintained that he was a victim of the *manie persécutrice*. This idiosyncrasy was intimately related to another which heightened the bitterness of Marat's feeling. He had a profoundly suspicious nature that made it difficult for him ever to credit an opponent with honest and sincere intentions. Sincere himself to the point of lacking a sense of humor and proportion, he always believed that any who differed from him in opinion were actuated by base and ulterior motives. When we find him, as we shall again and again, advocating measures which were almost universally opposed, replying with a wry cynicism to the epithets that are hurled against him, calling down fervid anathemas upon his enemies, and rejoicing when they come to grief, it is because his one-track mind could grasp but one side to any question, because he was always absolutely convinced of his own sincerity and infallibility and, therefore, of the insincerity and fallibility of those who disagreed with him. The result was that he constantly looked upon himself as a martyr in the cause of truth and honor, a victim of untruthful and dishonorable scoundrels. It is this combination of persecution mania and distrust of others' motives that more than any other psychological process furnishes the key to his character. For lack of a better name, let us call it his "martyr complex."

It was because of this martyr complex that, when he was unsuccessful in his attempt to gain admittance into the Academy of Sciences, he believed that every kind of prejudice was being brought to bear against him. He was quite sure that there could be no doubt as to his deserving the honor, but jealousy and an ignorant fear of accepting new scientific doctrines had stolen it from him. Even Brissot, writing his *Mémoires* at a time when there was every reason for him to be unjust to Marat, admitted that he had shared Marat's feeling in this matter; and there is extant a brochure entitled *De la Vérité*, in which Brissot attacked the Academy on behalf of his friend for its blind acceptance of obsolete Newtonianism to the exclusion of Marat's new discoveries. The truth is that while Marat's results were worthy of consideration, they were not as significant as he inordinately supposed. In so far as they attacked Newton's theories they were remarkable for boldness rather than truth and, in view of the relative estimation of the two scientists' merits to-day, justified the Academy in withholding the honors to which Marat felt he was entitled.

Marat's attitude toward the French Academy was made even more bitter when, in spite of all of his efforts, the possibility of becoming associated as Director with an academy of sciences at Madrid likewise failed to materialize. He had conducted an extensive correspondence on this subject with those who were in a position to help him attain this distinction. Several recently published letters in this correspondence reveal that Monsieur de Marat (it will be remembered that he claimed to be a descendant of a noble Spanish family) was willing to turn Spanish ("My heart has long been Spanish," he writes), to publish his *Theory of Medical Electricity*, crowned by a French academy, in Spain for the greater honor of his "future country," and—Calvinist though he was by birth and Deist though he was by preference—to simulate a "respect for the Holy Religion," in order to secure the position. But all to no avail. We learn from one of his admirers, a certain Philippe-Rose Roume, to whom these letters were addressed and who had helped to establish this Spanish Academy, that the opportunity was "stolen from him by the insidious manœuvres of his enemies." Bougeart, one of the biographers greatly biased in favor of Marat, claims that it was Bailly, already one of the most influential members of the French Academy, who was responsible for these "insidious manœuvres," but in view of the unreliability of our sources regarding them, it would be safer to assume that the honor was not forthcoming for less sensational reasons than the perfidy of Marat's enemies.

There is also good cause to believe that Marat, disappointed at this juncture, did not entirely abandon the pursuit for approbation and glory. Frederick the Great of Prussia was well-known as a liberal patron of the arts and sciences. Marat, moreover, had an additional claim upon his generosity as one of his subjects, having been born in Neuchâtel, at that time a possession of the Hohenzollerns. We have a letter, evidently addressed to someone high in the confidence of the King of Prussia, in which Marat practically begged for some token of Frederick's appreciation. But there is no evidence that Frederick ever took any notice of the request.

Marat never forgave the Academy of France, upon whom,
in at least two instances, he put the blame for these frustra-
tions. He believed himself to have rescued science from
chaos and to have placed it upon a solid foundation of method
and experimentation; he considered his work far superior to
Newton's; he admitted that his one and dominant passion was
the *"amour de la gloire"* and claimed that in general "the
source of every passion is the love of self." No wonder,
then, that his vain and sensitive spirit was grievously hurt
by this lack of recognition. The wound left in him a feeling
of deep resentment. Brissot was probably correct in his statement that Marat's subsequent research was undertaken largely
in the hope of confounding the Academy. But he proved
himself an unjust critic when he maintained that Marat in
his translation of Newton's *Opticks* had been guilty of a mean
dishonesty unworthy of one with even the slightest scholarly
pretensions. This translation appeared anonymously in 1787
under the editorship of Beauzée, one of the Forty of the
French Academy. Brissot believed or feigned to believe that
Marat had illegitimately inserted in it many of his own
ingenious ideas on the subject and that the Academy of
Science, relying upon the endorsement of Beauzée, a gram-
marian who probably knew very little about science, gave
it its approval. But a collation of Marat's translations with
the original of Newton's *Opticks* is sufficient to prove that
Brissot's evident anxiety to be fair even to his enemies was
here unable to resist the strong temptation to be otherwise.
The translation has been faithfully executed. That certain
minor changes in the text had been made in order to im-
prove the style was pointed out not only by the translator
but by the editor. The translator was careful to indicate
which of the footnotes were his, and in a brief essay at the
end of the book he made some comments on the progress of
optics since Newton's day. Furthermore, it would appear

from Beauzée's introductory letter of presentation to the King
that the translator was entirely unknown to him and that he
had consented to sponsor the book only after it had already
been approved by the Academy of Sciences.   As a matter of
fact, it was Bailly and Rochon, scientists not likely to give
their support lightly, who reported on the translation for the
Academy of Sciences and urged its approval.   Brissot should
have known Marat better than to have concocted this story.
Marat took himself altogether too seriously to wish to bluff
his scientific attainments upon an unwilling world.   But it
is more than likely that the approval of a work of his that had
been protected by anonymity strengthened his belief that the
objections to him in the Academy were personal and not
scientific.   His rancor therefore remained unabated.   Later,
during his revolutionary career, he took every opportunity to
attack the members of the Academy individually and collectively.   This policy culminated in a pamphlet, published in
1791, entitled *Charlatans modernes ou lettres sur la charlatanisme académique*, his most vehement, though not his parting,
lashing.   But these were merely the ineffectual ragings of a
balked ambition and yielded no results; in the field where his
amour de la gloire had first found a chance for satisfaction, he
had experienced humiliating defeat.

True, he continued his work in science up to the very eve
of the Revolution, but there is a steady diminution both in
the number of his publications and in the seriousness of their
subjects.   In 1779–1780, the period during which he was being considered for the French Academy, he published three
works on fire, electricity, and light.   Then came his first re-
buff, followed by two years in which no production of his pen
appeared.   Afterwards, between 1782 and 1784, the years in
which his hopes were buoyed up by the possibility of association with the Spanish Academy, he published three more
volumes, two on electricity and one on optics.   But from

1784 to 1789, a period of about five years following his second
failure, only four publications of his were issued from the
press, and only one of these—*Mémoires académiques ou nouvelles découvertes sur la lumière* (1788)—was of a serious
nature. Of the other three, the first (1785) was a reply of
thirty-three pages, which Marat facetiously called *Observations de l'amateur Avec*, to a certain Abbé Sans who had attacked his theories on electricity; the second (1785) was a
brief article on aeronautics, called forth by a recent balloon
catastrophe which had resulted in the death of two persons;
the third (1787) was the translation of Newton's *Opticks*
that he has been accused of having altered to conform to his
own ideas. This striking difference between both the number and the nature of his studies before and after the destruction of his hopes may be entirely fortuitous, but when linked
with what we know of Marat's self-confessed passion for
glory and his martyr complex, it leads to the inference that
his interest in science was waning toward the end of this dec-
ade. He was ready, even eager, to start off on the conquest of new worlds, and when another field was opened, he
devoted himself to it more thoroughly, more whole-heartedly,
than other professional men who were called to play their
rôles in the French Revolution.

It is not difficult to imagine what would have been the
result if Marat had obtained the coveted seat in the Academy. During the years preceding the Revolution, instead
of being a man nursing a grudge, he would have gone on living contentedly in the prestige thus bestowed upon him.
Had he taken any part in the Revolution at all, then, it
would probably have been in the moderate and contained manner that characterized the activities of Academicians such
as Bailly, Condorcet, and Lavoisier. There is every reason
to believe that he would have been entirely conservative and
well-satisfied with the world, and not a sensitive soul touched

to the quick by an alleged injustice.   As things actually were, however, the Revolution offered him a new outlet for his pent-up *amour de la gloire*.   Subconsciously, or perhaps even consciously, he now turned whatever genius he had, or thought he had, from science, which had proved sterile, to the opportunities offered by the impingements of events culminating in the French Revolution.

Until the Revolution, then, Marat, though a man of varied interests, had devoted himself chiefly to science; his dilettanteism in politics was incidental and almost accidental. On the whole, but for one or two facts, his career and associations had been of the kind to make him conservatively inclined.   If things had gone well during the Revolution, his conservative spirit might still have triumphed.   But, on the other hand, he had borrowed some of the most radical ideas of contemporary thinkers; and, furthermore, his ambition for a career as a man of science had been thwarted.   For these reasons he was dissatisfied and a background for radicalism was set for him.   As yet his feelings were amorphous.   It required a sense of complete despair with circumstances as he was to find them to bring out his more radical nature.   But radicalism and conservatism are essentially matters of temperament rather than conviction, and in one of Marat's peculiar temperament, it was not difficult to inspire radicalism.

CHAPTER II

MARAT, we have seen, was not born a Frenchman, but he so soon adopted France as his *patrie* that we may regard him as a fair representative of the French *bourgeois d'autrefois*. It was this bourgeois class that was to be the prime mover of the early political reforms of the Revolution. It was this bourgeois class that felt itself most aggrieved because of the monopoly of political privileges and honors by the nobility and clergy, because of its inability to control a government whose instability threatened business conditions, because of its having to shoulder the greater part of the burden of taxation, even while it had grown in numbers, wealth, learning, and power. It was from this bourgeois class that the great reforming philosophers—Voltaire, Rousseau, Helvétius, Diderot, and others—came and to whom especially they addressed their works. Marat was only one of millions who were able to cite and recite eloquent passages from their writings and only one out of probably hundreds who tried to emulate their example.

At first, as we shall see, he was little concerned with the lower classes save in a perfunctory sort of way, as became a political philosopher. For that matter, few of the writers of the Period of Enlightenment except the Physiocrats were interested in the peasant. When finally Marat did become the leader of the populace, his thoughts were not for the dwellers in the country, but for the city worker—not yet a factory hand in France, but an artisan or a shop employee.

Except when he adopted the loose talk about distribution of land that was fashionably current in his time, he gave no thought to peasants. Having lived in cities all his life, he did not know the peasant.

Yet the peasant class was the most wretched of all of the sufferers of the chaotic government and society of the Ancient Regime. He owed dues to the government, to his lord, to the church—in kind, in labor, in money. Taine has estimated—perhaps with gross exaggeration—that he paid eighty-one per cent of his income in the form of taxes and feudal dues of one sort or another. While there were more peasant landowners now than ever before, it was they who more than the serfs or the *métayers* or the free laborers felt the burden of the dues that even freeholders were required to pay their seigniors. The right of the lords to hunt upon their lands and in so doing destroy their crops weighed more heavily upon those who owned the entire harvest they produced than upon share-croppers or serfs. In all this Marat was only superficially interested. He was a city-man; he had no following in the rural districts; when he ceased to be a leader of the bourgeoisie, he became a leader of the working-class.

When Marat was born, Louis XV sat upon the throne of France. This prodigal king had inherited a huge war debt from his predecessor Louis XIV. An attempt of the Regency during his minority to become wealthy overnight by the reckless gambling of John Law had only increased this debt. Louis XV, by his extravagance at home, by his stupid policy abroad, through which he lost three wars and a vast colonial empire, paid little attention to the depletion of his treasury. It would last as long as he, and after that the deluge! Louis XVI, who had to face the deluge, was obliged to call upon his subjects for their aid, and the French Revolution was on.

Marat had lived in France only a short time during the

reign of Louis XV and then only as a student. This explains his silence on the old profligate and the abuses of his reign. He had lived in England until 1777 and knew more about George III's digressions and the weaknesses of the English constitution. But all of the facts that we have discussed were bound to exert their influence upon him when he again took up his French allegiance. They made the Revolution, which made Marat, who in turn helped make the Revolution.

When the vacillating but well-meaning Louis XVI succeeded to the throne that his debauched predecessor had bequeathed him, he tried earnestly to play the part of the enlightened despot that so well became his contemporaries, Frederick of Prussia, Catherine of Russia, Joseph of Austria, and others. One of his first acts was to call Turgot, philosopher and statesman, into his ministry as Controller-General of Finances. Turgot made several important reforms, but in doing so, rendered himself unpopular with powerful influences at court and was soon obliged to resign. For a short time the incapable Clugny took charge of finances in his stead, but upon Clugny's death the King called in Necker, in whom the business men of France had the utmost confidence. Necker's fate, however, was much like Turgot's and in 1781 he too resigned. Joly de Fleury and D'Ormesson followed each other in quick succession until in 1783 Calonne was named Minister of Finances. For a few years Calonne was able to carry on the government by means of loans and lotteries, but when he proposed new taxes, the *Parlement* of Paris, one of thirteen bodies that alone had anything like a restrictive power upon the king's decrees, refused to register them. Calonne, therefore, proposed the calling of a Council of Notables, a body of the leading celebrities of the realm that had not been called together since 1626, to discuss the financial status of the country. The Notables met on February 22, 1787, did nothing except to force the dismissal of Calonne, and adjourned on May 25, 1787.   Brienne, the Archbishop of Sens, who had been one of his leading opponents among the Notables, succeeded him as Minister of Finances.

Miniature revolutions were already in progress in several provinces, and particularly in Dauphiny, where the redoubtable Mounier arose as the champion of constitutional reform. So chaotic was the financial and political condition of the state that autocracy had to confess its inability to cope with the situation and called upon the people for their co-operation. Brienne was obliged to decide that the obsolete Estates-General, a representative body that had not been convened for a hundred and seventy-five years, would have to be revived.   Consequently there was issued the *Arrêt du Conseil* of July 5, 1788, stating that the King intended to convoke the Estates-General and urging *"tous les savants et personnes instruits"* of the kingdom to send to the Guard of the Seals the reports of their investigations into the history and nature of that organization, which had practically ceased to exist since 1615.   The King declared that on the basis of these reports he would regulate the procedure of the forthcoming meeting of the representatives of the people, "in order to make the assembly as national and as general as it ought to be." On August 8, 1788, the date of May 1, 1789 was set for the first meeting of the rejuvenated national legislature.

The invitation to the educated men of France to investigate and write upon the Estates-General had in the meantime met with a general response, and the country was flooded with monographs and disputations on what the Estates-General were and what they ought to be.   As a result of these came the famous *Résultat du Conseil* of December 27, 1788—the "New Year's gift" of Necker, who had been recalled to take Brienne's place in the crisis.   Its most important provision fixed the representation of the Third Estate, which included all those who were neither clericals, or of the First Estate, nor nobles, or of the Second Estate, at a number equal to that of the other two orders combined. This was greeted as a radical and highly commendable concession by a benevolent King, although the nobles and clergy contained within their ranks probably no more than three hundred thousand souls altogether, while the Third Estate included over twenty-four millions. Shortly after the *Résultat du Conseil* the manner of electing the deputies to the Estates-General was regulated in the *Lettres Royales* of January 24, 1789. During all this time the admiration of the French for Louis XVI and his government had reached a point of warm enthusiasm. Everywhere the hope was expressed that a new era of political freedom and happiness had dawned for France.

Among those who had contributed to the flood of literature on the Estates-General was Jean Paul Marat. The memoirs of both Brissot and Lafayette state that Marat took no part in the Revolution before the fall of the Bastille, but, as we shall see, their statements are not true and may be attributed to the frailty of human memory or even to malice aforethought. For from the very beginning Marat took an active, though not prominent, part in the revolutionary movement. During the period between the *Arrêt du Conseil* of July 5, 1788 and the *Lettres Royales* of January 24, 1789, he was, he informs us, dangerously ill and daily expecting to breathe his last. To have died without having had a share in the prologue of the Revolutionary drama, without having given expression to his *amour de la gloire* in the new field of opportunity, would have been a miserable death indeed. And so he put forth what he expected to be his last efforts in the composition of a work dramatically entitled *Offrande à la Patrie*. Although this was published in February 1789, it seems to have been written before the *Lettres Royales* of January 24.

In this pamphlet the writer indicated that he shared the

feeling of hopeful expectation that prevailed about him. Louis XVI, he declared, was a good king, characterized by "his love for his people, his zeal for the public welfare." The noble monarch, roused by the mismanagement of his ministers and the infidelities of the nobility and the clergy, had turned to his people for guidance. For love of him France must put forth her best efforts to meet the emergency: "Blessed be the best of kings!" And Necker, the much hated and feared Necker of later days, was now no less esteemed. For the moment he was "the great statesman, equally distinguished for the sagacity of his views and the spotlessness of his career, whose talents have called him to the administration of finances." With such a king and such a minister, Marat took it for granted that the government of France ought to be monarchical.

He had studied his Montesquieu very carefully, however, and was entirely convinced of the necessity of keeping the legislative, judiciary, and executive branches of the government separate and distinct. He wanted the legislative power, of course, to belong exclusively to the Estates-General, but, on account of the complexity of a great kingdom such as France, he felt that they ought to exercise this power only in questions of national and general interest. The king's province was to act as the executive power, which was to include the administration of the laws and of internal affairs, jurisdiction over foreign policy, and the making of appointments. The judicial power he wished to see confided to a hierarchy of tribunals, of which the court of last resort in both civil and criminal cases was to be the King's Council. This first court of justice of the realm was also to try impeachments upon the indictment of a committee from the Estates-General, the king having no power to pardon or to prevent the trials of officials under impeachment. By making the branches of the government independent of each other in this way, Marat hoped to create a system of checks and balances which would prevent the accumulation of too much power in any one of the three departments.

Marat believed that, together with these regulations for the trichotomy of governmental powers, the fundamental laws of the kingdom ought to include a declaration of the rights of man. Among these rights of man he emphasized especially the freedom of press, which, when censored, favored the despotism of the Academy; the right of habeas corpus; a more equitable court procedure, which should include trial by jury, public sessions of courts, and lawyers at government expense for the poor; no exemption from taxation, which should be in proportion to wealth; the abolition of hunting rights; and a more just and humane criminal code. There was very little of an original nature in Marat's book. These were popular demands that he was only one among thousands to agitate for.

His conception of the fundamental laws of France would have provided for little better than a slightly limited despotism, in view of the tremendous powers left by it in the hands of the king and the restricted sphere of legislation granted to the Estates-General. Marat, however, disciple of Rousseau as well as of Montesquieu as he was, had not repudiated his belief in the sovereignty of the people. He was beginning to conceive of the people as the great mass of peasants and workers, who now, on the eve of a colossal revolution, were enjoying the support of the financiers, the newly created nobles, the curés, and the men of letters. He implied that these higher classes were not of the people, but merely allied to it temporarily, and that there was imminent danger of their being detached from it by the enemies of the Third Estate. However, this alliance of classes, which made up the body of the nation, was for him the only true sovereign; from it alone emanated all legitimate authority. He looked to it, and more particularly to the upper strata of it, to take the direction of

the Revolution into its own hands and, co-operating with the
King, to achieve a reformation of French society and government that should be for the benefit of the entire nation.   The
kingship, he repeated, was instituted only to force observance
of the laws; the king himself was subject to them.   If the
government should refuse to accept the constitution that was
about to be proposed, the nation had the right to resort to decisive means to force it to do so by refusing all aid to the
state, by preventing the levying of taxes, and by meting out
justice to offenders on its own authority.   In the last analysis,
therefore, Marat felt that the body of the people was the
judge of what the constitution ought or ought not to be.   He
was confident, however, that no duress of any nature would
have to be exercised upon the "wise and virtuous ministry" of
France.

If we are to believe Marat, this brochure created a sensation
and was crowned by one of the patriotic societies with which
France teemed at this time.   That it was thus crowned there
seems to be no reason to deny: there were too many societies
that had acquired the crowning habit to make it at all improbable.   But there seems to have been very little in it to create
any more of a sensation than hundreds of other pamphlets of
the same kind.   At any rate, Marat felt constrained to publish a *Supplément de l'*OFFRANDE À LA PATRIE.   This made
its appearance in April 1789 and was evidently composed after
the *Lettres Royales* of January 24 had been published.   The
tone of these letters had displeased Marat.   He sought in
vain, he said, for "the simple and true tone of a tender father
who desires only the welfare of his children," and found instead "the too ordinary language of an imperious Prince whose
affairs are in disorder and who is willing to receive the petitions of his subjects, provided that they grant him, in their
turn, the means of getting out of difficulty."   Disillusioned
and disappointed, he cried;

It is not the public disasters and the pitiful groans of his subjects
reduced to despair that disturb his tranquillity; it is the exhaus-
tion of his treasury that takes from him his peace of mind.

If, however, Marat felt that there had been a change of
attitude at the court, it was the King's ministers and not the
King himself whom he held responsible.   His faith in Louis
XVI remained constant and offered to him a ray of hope.   He
still regarded the King as "a tender and generous father" to
his subjects.   "No," he said, "there yet is virtue on the throne.
Good faith, truth, justice have placed their sanctuary in the
soul of Louis XVI."   Marat was sure that such a prince could
not desert his people.   For Necker, too, though he was afterwards to maintain that his first revulsion of feeling toward
that statesman came as a result of the Letter of Convocation,
he still had the high regard that he had formerly entertained.
For had not Necker managed his office well, despite the opposition of the higher orders?

Nevertheless, there was no denying that the government's
position had changed and that something must be done about
it.   The method of procedure that Marat now proposed in
view of what seemed to be the new purpose of the administration was to reject the privilege of drawing up *cahiers*, the lists
of grievances that the King had called for in his *Lettres
Royales*, and to insist that the deputies of the people act
solemnly and earnestly with the King, resolved not to adjourn
until they had completed their task of framing a constitution
for France.   In the meantime, the people must concede
neither aid nor taxes to the government.   With regard to the
problems of the composition of the Estates-General—an
issue which more than any other was then agitating the French
nation—he fell in with the proposals of all the other champions of the Third Estate.   The issue was whether each
deputy to the Estates-General was to have a vote equal to
that of any other deputy, regardless of which of the three

Estates he represented, or whether each of the three Estates was to have but one vote determined by the majority of its members.   It was obvious that in the latter case the two upper houses, the Clergy and the Nobility, would vote together and defeat any proposals of the Third Estate.   But if each representative had one vote, the fact that the Third Estate comprised as many deputies as the other two together would give it control of the balloting.   Marat, of course, fell in with the advocates of reform.   He urged that the Estates General meet as a single body and not as three separate orders, with vote by head and not by order.   Since the Third Estate were in favor of a new and liberal constitution, while the First and Second Estates on the whole proposed simply the confirmation of the old institutions and traditions of France, the vote by head would mean a victory for the reformers.   As to the fundamental laws to be embodied in the new constitution, Marat had no further suggestions to make in his new book, but he repeated his emphasis upon the necessity of keeping the legislative, executive, and judiciary branches distinct and separate.   For the sake of expediency, however, he was willing to concede to the first prince of the royal house or to the first officer of the crown the presidency of the Estates General. Another concession, surprising in view of his later stand on the veto power, is his declaration that

> if the constitution leaves to the king any share in the legislative power, it ought to be only in the right to approve or to reject the laws which are passed, as is the practice today among the English.

Although he had quite evidently been piqued by the government's more candid policy in the *Lettres Royales* and had, in his displeasure, written the *Supplément de l'*OFFRANDE À LA PATRIE, it presented no new radical program, but merely urged certain precautions in order to prevent the emasculation of the Revolution.

The popularity of these pamphlets was probably not as great as Marat induced himself to believe. It is true that the views which they contained were, as he affirmed, "consecrated in almost all the *cahiers* of the deputies of the Estates," but there is no reason to believe that this was due any more to the influence of Marat than to that of many another who had voiced similar ideas. In fact, from the date of the publication of the *Supplément de l'*OFFRANDE À LA PATRIE until May 5, 1789, when the Estates General formally opened its sessions—a period during which his importance, if it was as great as he maintained, ought to have made itself more clearly felt—Marat's activities were very limited. They were restricted to his duties as a member of the electoral committee of the District of the Carmes Déchaussés, one of the sixty divisions of Paris organized for the purpose of choosing the deputies to represent the Third Estate of the capital in the Estates General. What Marat did as an elector or for whom he cast his votes, we do not know. But he held this position until September 1789 and resigned only to devote himself to the publication of his journal. An anonymous brochure on the *Vie privée de J. P. Marat* assures us that he was among those who brought about the defection of the French Guards, a military unit that played the leading part in the disorders of July 1789, but this statement is otherwise unconfirmed.

In the meantime the Estates General had encountered a series of memorable crises. Its first meeting had taken place on May 5, 1789 in the presence of the King, the Queen, and the royal ministers. Nothing definite was said regarding the burning question of the manner of voting, although vague intimations that the vote by order ought to be permitted to the conservative Estates were made. From that day until June 27 the Third Estate, therefore, found itself pitted against the King and the upper two Estates in a struggle over the question of vote by head versus vote by order. On June 27 the King was obliged to yield and to order the Nobles and Clergy to meet with the Commoners. Vote by head thus was granted legitimacy and the royal sanction. The Estates General became in fact the National Assembly. In it the Third Estate predominated, and bent every effort toward making France a limited monarchy.

But in July, the conservative or court party, led by the Queen and Marat's one-time patron, the Count of Artois, induced the all too easily influenced King to gather an armed force at Versailles with the intention of using it against the National Assembly. On July 11, Necker, the leader of the liberal faction in the Royal Council and the idol of the French people, was dismissed. In fear that the revolutionary movement which was meant to benefit them would be suppressed, the Paris populace, for the first time, took an active part in the political drama of the Revolution. On July 14, the Hôtel des Invalides and the Bastille were attacked. The former fell without offering any telling opposition. The other was taken only after a bloody struggle; the commander and a few soldiers of the garrison were massacred after its surrender. This event caused the King to recall Necker and to dismiss the troops who had been mobilized at Versailles. On July 17 he went himself to Paris, there to put on the tricolor cockade as a token of submission. The Paris mob had prevented reaction.

Marat, despite his efforts to glorify his rôle, played but a small part in the stirring events of the Fall of the Bastille. He published a statement, characteristically exaggerated, to the effect that he had detected an attempt of a large body of royal cavalry to march into Paris under the pretense of bringing aid to the people but with the real intention of turning it over to slaughter during the night. Confirmatory testimony, not derived from Marat's own account of the event, is wholly lacking, although he claimed that there were many witnesses to it.   It would not be safe, therefore, to credit the story altogether.   Indeed, Brissot, who published the original narrative of the episode in his journal, later called it an absolute fiction.   Yet it would be just as unsafe to reject Marat's report entirely.   For not only is Brissot's memory untrustworthy, as we have already had occasion to see, but there is some small evidence, though of a negative nature, to support Marat's account.   He named at least one witness, Broussais de la Grey of the Paris Commune, who never denied the statement, although he had good reason to do so when Marat later attacked his personal integrity.   The truth seems to be that Marat, who never had a sense for numbers anyway, was making a mountain out of a molehill; he had probably caused the arrest of a few royal cavalry on that day, immediately exaggerating their number into an army and assigning murderous counter-revolutionary motives to their activities. A year later, in an excoriation of Necker, he claimed to have spent all of the next forty-eight hours with the Committee of the Carmes Déchaussés, in expectation of some act of royal retribution.   After he had taken some much needed rest and the crisis had passed, he came to the conclusion that his sphere of activity lay in the journalistic world rather than in the occupations of a commissioner of a district.   It was then that he conceived of the idea of establishing a newspaper.

His first attempt to carry this idea into execution came shortly after.   The events of the Fourteenth of July had given impetus to the work of the National Assembly on the proposed constitution.   As it became more and more evident that the first Committee of the Constitution under the leadership of Mounier was intending to give to France a document modeled upon that of England, Marat's old feeling regarding the imperfection of that instrument of government returned and found expression in letters that he sent to the most famous of the Constituents.   He claimed to have written twenty such missives, but there is only one extant today, affixed to his French edition of the *Chains of Slavery*, under the title of *Tableau des vices de la Constitution anglaise*. It is dated August 23, 1789. In it Marat spoke against the plan of Mounier's committee, maintaining that the English constitution had several vices and emphasizing especially the influence of the king upon legislation. With like purpose in mind he began his first journal which was entitled *Le Moniteur patriote*. But though this periodical ran to forty numbers, Marat was associated with only its first issue.

As time passed, the date for the report of the Committee of the Constitution drew constantly nearer. The questions that exercised the Assembly and the people of Paris most were whether there should be an upper house in the legislature and whether the king should have the right to veto legislation. An affirmative answer to both of these questions would strengthen the aristocracy greatly; a negative one might destroy it entirely. If Marat was to make his views on the constitution count for anything, it behooved him to put them before the public speedily. This he did in a work named *La Constitution ou Projet de déclaration des Droits de l'homme et du citoyen, suivi d'un Plan de constitution juste, sage et libre*, which appeared toward the end of August 1789. The author had evidently intended the book to be published earlier. At any rate, in the preface, he apologized for its late appearance, claiming that it had been ready for the press three weeks earlier, but that printers and police regulations had interfered with its immediate issue. It was frankly intended to influence public opinion and the vote of the Assembly upon the proposals of Mounier.

Here Marat shows himself to have been an eclectic political philosopher, building his theories again upon what pleased him most especially from Montesquieu and Rousseau. From the latter he took once more the theory of the sovereignty of the people that he had used before. Members of the state, he wrote, engage in a social contract for their mutual interest. Taken individually, therefore, the people are subjects; taken collectively, they are the sovereign. As sovereign they are entirely independent of every human power, their acts are law, and they are the only true legislature. However, for reasons of practicality, the people act through representatives. Birth alone gives every citizen the right to share in the selection of these representatives. The national senate, thus chosen by universal suffrage, becomes the central authority of the state, but its decrees do not become law until they have been sanctioned by the people; and lest it should grow too powerful, its individual members are subject to recall and punishment. Thus Marat appeared to advocate a unicameral legislature, subject to the direction and good-will of its constituencies. The army, too, he argued, ought to be faithful first to the people and then to the king; it ought to be a national militia under the orders of municipal magistrates rather than an armed force dependent upon and bound by oath to the ruler.

To strengthen this doctrine of the sovereignty of the people, Marat borrowed from Montesquieu the theory of the separation of powers, which he likewise had advocated before. Like most of the political writers of his day, he considered France too large and its administration too complex to be adapted to anything but a monarchical form of government. Care must be taken, however, to circumscribe the power of the monarch, so as to prevent him from becoming tyrannical. Arguing again that even in England the legislative and executive branches were not sufficiently separated, he urged that the defects of the English constitution be avoided—that the king be deprived of all means of influencing elections, that the legislature be permitted to convene and adjourn of its own accord without the intervention of the executive, and that no one who should sit in the law-making body be allowed to accept any office from the crown until after the lapse of ten years.

As we have seen, Marat had championed these limitations upon the royal prerogative before, but in this work he insisted upon others here suggested for the first time. He wished to take all significance from the right of veto, which he formerly had been willing to grant to the king. Now he wanted it to be merely a formality, the king consenting as a matter of course to every bill that had been passed by the legislature. Furthermore, in order to prevent the executive power from exerting too great an authority over the judiciary, Marat thought that the right to nominate judges ought to belong to the municipalities. His purpose in thus limiting the influence of kings was "not to demand of them that they do good" but to "make it impossible for them to do harm."

Eloquent as were some of these expositions, his most appealing tones were reserved for a plea for greater social justice. The misery of the poor and unfortunate still moved Marat. He saw them, often the victims of circumstances and mischance beyond their control, striving in vain to better their humble lot or resigning themselves in utter despair to their wretchedness. By nature, he cried, they were born subject to certain needs and from these needs alone they derived their rights to satisfaction. Should society deny them these rights, they might justly obtain them by force. To preserve their own lives and to resist oppression they might even take the lives of others. Therefore, to maintain peace, society ought to forbid by law the growth of conspicuous inequalities of wealth. Society owed to its members who owned no property a means of subsistence, while, on the other hand, those who possessed only their physical necessities, if so much, owed nothing to society. It was from those who had more than enough that the state ought to collect its revenue. He even went so far as to avow that where marked differences in wealth existed, a part at least of the property of the rich, often become opulent through intrigue and dishonesty, ought to be confiscated for the amelioration of the condition of the needy.

This book presented with greater thoroughness the familiar line of reasoning that Marat had already developed; and along with it occurred repetitions of the same contradictions that he had previously been guilty of. For example, while seeking to circumscribe the royal power, he left to the king not only the right to issue administrative ordinances, which were to have effect as long as the legislature allowed, but also the prerogative of appointing his ministers, who, however, were not to retain office in the face of public opinion. Again, while declaiming against the injustice of private wealth, he maintained that the right of private property was a necessary factor in civil liberty; and while declaring that birth alone gave one the right of suffrage, he believed that women and children ought to take no part in political affairs since they are adequately represented by the heads of the family. Moreover, he declared that where the worth of candidates for office was equal, the representatives of the people ought to be elected from the richer classes of citizens, their fortunes being a guarantee of their good behavior. In other words, he was not a socialist in any modern sense of the word, although he did perceive, as he already had even before the Revolution, that the unequal distribution of wealth was unjust and reprehensible. Up to this point the general tenor of Marat's early publications had become successively more radical and his political philosophy more definite and organized, but it was evident that he was still expectant of a revolution which should take place without any violent change in the government of France. He wished that the power of the king should be limited, but that France should continue to be a monarchy in more than name alone. The monarch, to be sure, was to be enlightened, to undertake measures for the welfare of the poor, to seek to better the condition of his subjects, but he was still to be left tremendous powers that he might use for evil as well as for good. Whatever reform was to take place, then, was to seep down from above and not to rise from below.

This conception of the Revolution was continued in the first issues of the *Ami du Peuple*. We have already seen that the first indication of Marat's intentions to found such a journal came while he was still a member of the electoral assembly of the District of the Carmes Déchaussés. Convinced of the necessity of a paper which would keep the electorate informed of the latest political developments, he originally wanted the electoral assembly to undertake its publication. Being unable, however, to persuade his colleagues to take such a step, he soon withdrew from that body in order to devote himself to the task alone. At first the heading of the journal led one to suspect that it was sponsored by a "society of patriots," but after a few issues had appeared, Marat openly avowed his sole responsibility for it. He soon projected his personality into the *Ami du Peuple* so completely that for contemporaries and for posterity he himself became known as the Friend of the People and his identity became inseparable from that of his journal. The prospectus of the leaflet made its appearance early in September 1789. The journal resembled in substance our American editorial page rather than a modern newspaper, seldom running to more than eight octavo pages and almost never giving the news except as a basis for editorial opinion. The first regular number was issued on September 12. Its title at the beginning was *Le Publiciste parisien*, but after the first five editions it took the more descriptive name of *L'Ami du Peuple*.

We shall return to the *Ami du Peuple* and we shall see that the establishment of this journal marked a turning-point in Marat's career; but in the early numbers he was still intent upon a revolution, to be achieved through the co-operation of the King and the bourgeois Assembly, which was to leave France a limited constitutional monarchy. When the Assembly voted the inviolability of the royal person and the indivisibility and heredity of the throne, his only objection was that the prerogatives of the crown had been established before the rights of the people had been considered. Even while remonstrating against the powers which, upon the enforced resignation of the first Committee of the Constitution, the second Committee on the Constitution proposed to vest in the king, he declared that the monarch ought to have the honors of sovereignty, such as the command of the army outside of the state, jurisdiction over the coinage of money, the making of treaties, and the sending and receiving of ambassadors. In other words, a large part of the administration of war, foreign affairs, and finance—three of the most important provinces of government,—he was still willing to leave in the hands of the ruler. Although even in the earliest numbers of the *Ami du Peuple* it was obvious that he was beginning to lose faith in the King's ministry, Louis himself again became the subject of a eulogy from his pen when the royal bodyguard was disbanded. Even Lafayette, for whom Marat later could find no invective hostile enough, met with enthusiastic praise when he refused to accept a large sum of money put at his disposal.

It appears, then, that until September 1789 Marat held many of the ideas conventionally mouthed by the majority of the contemporary intelligentsia. Although, as a liberal monarchist, he desired to restrict the king's power, he had no wish to see monarchy actually abolished or even rendered *fainéant*. Marat's position at this juncture was unsettled and shifting. Consistency is, after all, a virtue of the unimaginative mediocre and Marat was not that. But through all his inconsistencies the bourgeois approach to political philosophy is easily discernible.   His appeal is to the middle class; he has not yet conceived of the revolution as a popular movement.   "One might say," declares Jaurès, "that he called the proletariat to the rescue only in despair at seeing the normal plan of the Revolution disrupted by the stupidity of the moderate bourgeoisie."   It is this "despair at seeing the normal plan of the Revolution disrupted by the stupidity of the moderate bourgeoisie"—despair at what Marat soon was able to persuade himself was the counter-revolution —that henceforth troubled the suspicious spirit of the new-born Friend of the People and determined his future development.

CHAPTER III

ON certain occasions Marat sought to depict himself as a naïve, unsophisticated creature who did not know the manner or the value of deceiving his readers; and several of his more gullible biographers have endorsed this estimate at its face value. For them every comment in Marat's works has been the truth, told without embellishment or subterfuge. On the other hand, it has been held with equal ardor that nothing Marat said was worthy of unquestioning belief. Indeed, Marat often lied, often planned to mislead by false implication, often employed innuendo where directness and candor might have been unwise. But at times there was an engaging frankness about him which excites admiration. Particularly in describing his own attitude toward events, when it was a question of opinion rather than fact that was under discussion, was this true. Thus one of the most valuable statements on the change that now took place in Marat's career comes from his own journal at a time (March 19, 1793) when he was defending himself from the mordant reproaches of his enemies:

> At the outbreak of the Revolution, wearied by the persecutions that I had experienced for so long a time at the hands of the Academy of Sciences, I eagerly embraced the occasion that presented itself of defeating my oppressors and attaining my proper position. I came to the Revolution with my ideas already formed, and I was so familiar with the principles of high politics that they had become commonplaces for me. Having had greater confidence in the mock patriots of the Constituent Assembly than they deserved, I

was surprised at their pettiness, their lack of virtue. Believing that they needed light, I entered into correspondence with the most famous deputies, notably with Chapelier, Mirabeau, and Barnave. Their stubborn silence on all my letters soon proved to me that though they needed light, they cared little to be enlightened. I adopted the course of publishing my ideas by means of the press. I founded the *Ami du Peuple*. I began it with a severe but honest tone, that of a man who wishes to tell the truth without breaking the conventions of society. I maintained that tone for two whole months. Disappointed in finding that it did not produce the entire effect that I had expected, and indignant that the boldness of the unfaithful representatives of the people and of the lying public officials was steadily increasing, I felt that it was necessary to renounce moderation and to substitute satire and irony for simple censure. The bitterness of the satire increased with the number of mismanagements, the iniquity of their projects and the public misfortunes. Strongly convinced of the absolute perversity of the supporters of the old regime and the enemies of liberty, I felt that nothing could be obtained from them except by force. Revolted by their attempts, by their ever-recurrent plots, I realized that no end would be put to these except by exterminating the ones guilty of them. Outraged at seeing the representatives of the nation in league with its deadliest enemies and the laws serving only to tyrannize over the innocent whom they ought to have protected, I recalled to the sovereign people that since they had nothing more to expect from their representatives, it behooved them to mete out justice for themselves. This was done several times.

In these words, Marat toward the end of his crowded life examined his revolutionary activities and their motives. Except for a natural tendency toward self-glorification, explicable if not justifiable in one of Marat's temper, the judgment is honest and draws an outline of his biography that the historian can do little better than fill in and elaborate upon. As he admits, it was only after he had tried several other ways of putting his views before the Assembly and the public that he finally resorted to the publication of a daily paper, the *Ami du Peuple*, which we have already encountered. The prospectus

of this leaflet announced that it was the intention of the editor
to watch the proceedings of the National Assembly and to set
himself up as a monitor of the people in order to judge the
work of the nation's representatives.   The fundamental idea
of the journal from its inception was that the National Assembly would bear watching in the interests of the great mass
of the common people.   Perhaps, as Marat explained above,
the failure of the leading figures of the Assembly to reply to
his letters had caused him to lose confidence in them and was
one of the factors in the establishment of the *Ami du Peuple*,
although he should have been able to perceive how preposterous it was of him to expect them to single out his letters (and
who was he at this time?) from the mass of correspondence
that they must have been receiving at the beginning of their
sessions.   But even if this seeming neglect was a factor in
Marat's new departure, it was only half the story.

It was in the midst of the discussion of the Mounier project
proposed by the first Committee of the Constitution, that the
newspaper of Marat made its début, and its initiation is as
much due to Marat's opposition to this proposal as to any
other cause.   Naturally, in its first issues, the *Ami du Peuple*
took its stand against the plan of the Anglophiles, as the supporters of Mounier who desired a constitution like that of England were termed, and hardly, to use Marat's phrase, in the
"severe but honest tone of a man who wishes to tell the truth
without breaking the conventions of society."   Marat lent
his influence to the leaders of the faction opposed to the double
chamber and the absolute veto, singling out from among
these for special commendation his future enemy Lanjuinais.
Even after the National Assembly had voted to grant the
king only a suspensive veto, Marat yet discerned in this
greatly restricted right of the executive to interfere in legislation an instrument by which Louis XVI was placed above
the representatives of the people and made the arbiter of the

law, capable of defeating the constitution itself. Thus when
the King delayed in sanctioning the glorious decrees of the
feverish night of August 4–5, which, passed in a memorable
wave of contagious enthusiasm, abolished serfdom and the
privileges of the nobility, clergy and favored towns of France,
Marat considered this an example of the despotic power that
the right to veto had created. In a bicameral legislature he
could perceive merely a waste of time, energy and money:
if the two houses agreed, there was no advantage in the existence of the second chamber, and if they disagreed, the only
result would be to deadlock the legislative machinery hopelessly. He likewise insisted upon the right of the legislature
to meet at fixed intervals independently of the will of the
executive. In general he opposed the haphazard manner in
which the Assembly was acting and insistently declared that
the proper method of procedure would have been to have established the rights of the citizen once and for all before having considered the privileges of the King. He feared that if
the work of the Assembly were suddenly to be called to a halt,
it would be found that the King's position had been fortified
without anything having been done to ameliorate the lot of
the people.

By the time these last protests were made, however, the
Mounier committee had met with failure and had resigned.
The proposed constitution would have made a feasible instrument of government, but it was opposed not only by
radicals like Marat, who felt that it was too conservative, but
by the conservatives of the Clergy and Nobility, of whom
some thought it too radical, while others believed it would
prove practicable and for that very reason, in the hopes that
the failure of the Revolution might lead to a restoration of
their privileged status, were unwilling to accept it. A second
Committee on the Constitution was appointed. This won the
approbation of the *Ami du Peuple*—at least at the beginning

of its existence. One of its first proposals—to take the power of making appointments in large part away from the king and to place it in the hands of the legislative body—met with an expression of unmitigated satisfaction from Marat; and after a unicameral legislature had been decided upon, he again pronounced his approval.

Here Marat's "sincere but honest tone" changed. It had had just about the two months' duration that he claimed for it. Not even during this period had his language been "that of a man who wishes to tell the truth without breaking the conventions of society." Whatever spirit of moderation Marat had once possessed had been exhausted in the pamphlets that had appeared before the establishment of the *Ami du Peuple*. If his journal contained any tinge of restraint it appeared in the earliest numbers alone, and even then seemed restrained only in comparison with the extravagant vituperation of his later issues.

The foundation of the *Ami du Peuple* was a milestone in the life of Jean Paul Marat. Having abandoned the hope which the first stages of the Revolution had inspired, he had undertaken the task of watching and censuring; and the more he watched and censured, the stronger grew the feeling that that was exactly what was needed and that it could not be done too vigorously or too often. It is the same feeling that we have already witnessed—a profound suspicion of all who differed from him in thought or action. The republican Robert, one of the few important contemporary figures who understood Marat, explained this peculiarity picturesquely if not entirely accurately: "His malady," he said, "consists in believing that he is the only patriot of France, and it is a delirium." With such a malady an honest but moderate tone was impossible for any length of time.

Nor must we forget that Marat was constantly seeking to give vent to his *amour de la gloire*—a passion that can so

easily be confused with *amour de la patrie*.   Perhaps he re-
gretted that circumstances had so conspired that he had not
been chosen a member of the Estates General that now as
the National Assembly was working to shape the future constitution of France.   He would then not have had to exert
his influence upon the representatives of the people only
through twenty or so unanswered letters to leading Constituents.   But since he had to remain but an onlooker, he must
have realized—subconsciously at least—that for one outside
the National Assembly it would be easier to cut a figure as a
stalwart opponent of real or alleged injustices than as either
a passive spectator or an active supporter of its efforts.   Certainly there was much to oppose.

Among the first to feel the censure of this self-appointed
"eye of the people," who believed his pen "more useful in the
defense of liberty than a whole army," was the Assembly of
the Representatives of the Commune of Paris.   On September 25 he was first called before that august body to answer
for his conduct, but after three appearances was permitted to
go unmolested for the time being.   His attacks on the Commune continued, however.   This was a time when Paris was
threatened with a shortage of food, for the harvest of 1788
had been scanty and that of 1789, though good, had not been
adequately distributed.   Marat, claiming that the distress of
the capital was due to the negligence and mismanagement of
the Commune, expressed his indignation in no uncertain terms.
He attacked especially its secretary, M. de Joly, who had been
reported to him as a grafter.   Though he later discovered his
mistake and apologized to De Joly in an open letter, his out-
bursts against the organization as a whole grew no less violent.   And in later days, when he revised the numbers of his
paper in preparation for a new edition, which never appeared,
he in no way softened the tones of his attack upon De Joly in
his manuscript notes and additions.

Early in October 1789 troubled rumors that there had been a royalist demonstration at the Court of Versailles and that the King again intended to mobilize his loyal troops against the National Assembly added to the panic that already existed because of the lack of food and the machinations of the ambitious Duke of Orleans, who sought to be his cousin's successor on the throne of France. On October 5, a crowd of Parisians, urged by the clamors of popular journalists, of whom Marat was not the least, started on their notorious march to Versailles, headed by a troop of women crying for bread and denouncing Queen Marie Antoinette and the King's ministers. It was only the timely interference of Lafayette and his National Guard and the devotion of the people to their King that saved the Queen and the Royal Household from serious harm the next morning. But again Louis XVI was forced to go to Paris, this time accompanied by his family; and thenceforth the "Baker, the Baker's wife, and the Baker's boy" were practically the prisoners of the hungry people of their own capital, who fondly imagined that their presence would create bread and political security.

True to his wary nature, Marat, in constant fear of treason, had been one of the first to be roused to suspicion of counter-revolution and to call for action against the court-party when the concentration of troops at Versailles had again been bruited abroad. Camille Desmoulins facetiously described his nervous energy in investigating the reports coming from the palace:

> Marat flies to Versailles, returns like a flash, makes alone as much noise as four trumpets on the last day of judgment, and cries to us: O Dead! Awaken!

While it is true, however, that Marat took a leading part in inciting the insurrection of October 5–6, there is no reason to believe that his influence at this time was very marked.

On the contrary, the demonstration in favor of Mirabeau on the "March" has been and may justly be taken to show that his opinions counted for very little on that occasion, for at no time did Marat have any great respect and admiration for "the little father," although he had not yet begun to assail him as bitterly as he was soon to do.

Shortly after the events of October 5–6 the Châtelet, the obsolescent police court of the Ancient Regime, began its persecution of Marat. For his seditious utterances of October 2–5, which were regarded as having instigated the March to Versailles, and for his incendiary language, directed by this time not only at the Commune of Paris but at Necker as well, a decree of outlawry was issued against him on October 8. Despite the support he received from the radical journalists and sections of Paris, Marat, for the first time in his career, which was soon to be punctuated at frequent intervals with periods of coerced recess, was forced into hiding. He remained concealed for about a month. The last number of his journal before he was obliged to seek protection in his hidden asylum and the first after he came forth were new attacks upon the Commune, which had had a hand in his misfortune. He announced his conviction that by reducing the number of the representatives in the municipal assembly, by taking care that they were not corrupt or corrupted, and by granting to the Districts that had elected them the right to recall undesirable representatives, that body would be considerably improved. For the four days following the resumption of his paper, he repeated his charges, accusing the Commune of responsibility for the famine and the recent decree of martial law, of attempts upon the independence of certain revolutionary Districts and of various other injustices.

During the period that Marat was thus castigating the Commune, he was likewise directing his philippics against Necker, whom he had formerly held in such high regard.

Marat perceived that the National Assembly was divided into two distinct parties. One of these, the democratic group, was eager to draw up a constitution which he felt would form the cornerstone of the political happiness of France, while the other, the aristocratic faction, sought by fair means and foul to re-establish the monarchy in all its pristine power and glory. Necker seemed to him to be not only in league with the latter, but actually the source of their most audacious schemes. It was Necker whom he held responsible for the King's statement that he would accept the Declaration of the Rights of Man only if the executive authority with all its former prerogatives were again vested in him. To Necker, too, he believed were due the reactionary movements of the court-party in the period preceding the insurrection of October 5–6, 1789. And Necker furthermore, he maintained, instead of attending to the financial difficulties of the state, as his duty required, had been aiding wheat profiteers and had himself engaged in questionable speculations with government funds.

Attempts were made by both the Commune of Paris and Necker's agents to put an end to Marat's opposition. At one time, Marat asserted, he had even been offered a huge bribe for his silence. When he refused to hold his tongue and continued his relentless diatribes, several attempts were made to arrest him. He went into hiding again. But in December he was found in his place of refuge at Versailles and made a prisoner. He was taken to the *Comité des Recherches*, one of the commune's agencies, where Lafayette, as Commander-in-Chief of the National Guard, took a hand in his cross-examination. Marat explained everything away on the grounds of his patriotic zeal and was soon given his liberty again. In January 1790, however, the Châtelet revived its decree of outlawry against him, for his tirades had by no means subsided. In retaliation, the District of the Cordeliers, already the seat of the radical elements of Paris under the leadership of the young lawyer Danton, put the journalist under its protection and helped him to hide from the authorities. Marat now changed his place of residence to No. 39 Rue des Fossés-Saint-Germain, the present Rue de l'Ancienne Comédie, close by the Monastery of the Cordeliers, which was now the headquarters of the radical Cordeliers group. An attempt to take him into custody on January 9 was defeated by his retreat; and on January 17, having been summoned to appear before the Mayor at the Hôtel de Ville to answer to various charges, he publicly defied the authorities in his journal. By this time the "Marat Affair," as this series of events had come to be called, claimed the attention not only of the Commune but of the National Assembly as well, the deputies of the people having undertaken to remonstrate with the District of the Cordeliers for its protection of the seditious Marat.

The attacks upon Necker reached their culmination in a separate volume, entitled *Dénonciation contre Necker.* The manuscript of this fulmination was ready for the press early in November, but though Marat had approached ten printers with it, he could find none willing to be responsible for its publication. He finally had to print it himself. It appeared on January 18, 1790. Four days later a final effort to capture the troublesome journalist was made. This time the police were determined that he should not escape and employed a large force to overawe his sympathizers and to effect his arrest. Marat, with his utter lack of any conception of numbers, exaggerated the force into a veritable army when he came to tell of his adventure. At one time he made it 12,000 men with cannon, at another 4,000 men, saying nothing about cannon, and estimated the cost of the expedition at 500,000 livres. Recent investigation, however, points to the conclusion that it probably consisted of about 300 men, certainly no more than 500, without cannon and at a correspondingly

low cost.[1] Through the interference of Danton and the
District of the Cordeliers, the police were delayed in debates
over legal technicalities while Marat made good his escape.
Nevertheless, his press was destroyed and his papers confiscated. He himself was coerced into a short period of hiding
in the vicinity of Paris and soon felt obliged to seek safety
in England. The *Affaire de Marat* thus came to a close,
but out of it developed the *Affaire de Danton*, for the young
lawyer had obstructed the police in the performance of their
duty, and the District of the Cordeliers had to print a public
explanation of its conduct. Thus Marat became the cause
of Danton's first important public appearance.

Marat remained in England until the following April.
During his stay he wrote several pamphlets. One of these
was an *Appel à la nation*, in which he gave a favorable interpretation of his own career leading up to his present sorry
position and attacked his old enemies, the Commune, the
Châtelet and Necker. The last two of this trio he believed
worthy of special attention. In a *Lettre contenant quelques
réflexions sur l'ordre judiciaire* he shook a figurative fist at
the Châtelet; and in a *Nouvelle Dénonciation contre M.
Necker*, he rendered it entirely evident that the recent persecutions visited upon him had not increased his respect for the
famous Minister of Finances. After a sojourn of less than
three months in England, he thought it safe to reappear in
Paris. Shortly after his return to France, Necker was obliged
to resign, but the antipathy against him that had arisen in
Marat's breast knew no surcease as long as the Friend of
the People lived.

Another early idol of Marat's who, like Necker, very soon

---

[1] Babut, *Une journée au District des Cordeliers*, in the *Revue historique*,
March 1903; Buchez and Roux, *Histoire parlementaires*, IV, pp. 293 ff.; for
Marat's figures, see *Appel à la nation*, pp. 38–44, and *Ami du Peuple*, no. 366,
February 9, 1791, p. 7.

fell from his pedestal was Lafayette. Marat believed him likewise to be connected with the aristocratic faction of the Assembly which was seeking to restore the despotic power of the King. But he was chiefly concerned with Lafayette's intentions regarding the National Guard, of which the General was Commander-in-Chief. He feared that "the divine Mottier, the hero of two worlds, the Restorer of Liberty," as he ironically dubbed Lafayette, was aiming to make of the Guard a tool in the hands of the King's henchmen. Wherever there was the least suspicion of a plot, there Marat beheld the hand of Lafayette, whether it was in the matter of a rumored abduction of Louis XVI or in the spread of propaganda among laborers engaged upon public works. This hostility, beginning in 1789 and continuing throughout 1790, reached its zenith in a long series of attacks extending over the three issues of the *Ami du Peuple* of April 26–28, 1791, and continued until Lafayette's desertion in August 1792. This was an event of which Marat had frequently warned his readers; and when it occurred, along with the consternation that he shared with everyone else who feared for the welfare of France, there must have been a tinge of gloating.

Others who met with severe criticism in the early numbers of the *Ami du Peuple* were Bailly and Mirabeau. His antagonism to the former was due to the fact that he was a member of the Academy of Sciences, a colleague of Lafayette, and the leader of the moderate Paris Commune. The feeling of confidence in Mirabeau which was universally entertained in France Marat did not share. The premature death of the popular orator left almost all of France save the Friend of the People in deep mourning. Marat rejoiced in the death of the famous deputy and called upon his fellow-citizens to rejoice with him. He believed Mirabeau to have been a stipendiary of the King, which at this time others suspected too and which later was discovered to have been the case.

Brissot would have it that Marat attacked all these men because he could not suffer anyone to be greater and more popular than himself.   There is something more than personal jealousy, however, in Marat's attitude toward his more famous contemporaries.   His "martyr complex" was busily at work again.   His journal had been his last attempt to win glory and his enemies had tried to suppress that too.   With all but complete success they had again attempted to thwart his quest of free play for his ambition.   He probably felt himself persecuted for righteousness' sake and determined that no one who had attacked him must go unpunished. Personal feeling naturally entered into the matter.   But after all, it has never been difficult even for more honest people than Marat to mingle a personal cause with a great movement, to be unable, despite the best intentions, to distinguish between individual interest and public advantage, to believe sincerely that others who happened to quarrel with them on purely personal grounds were dangerous opponents of the popular movements they represented.   And, after all, whatever other explanation there is for Marat's attitude, it must be admitted that his diatribes were very often deserved.

To be sure, Marat did choose as a butt for his gibes those who were most in the public eye and of whom he was the most likely therefore to be jealous.   But, for that matter, any other champion of the people, self-appointed or not, would have acted in a similar way.   Prominence exposes one to criticism in proportion to the degree of one's popularity.   It would have been foolish for Marat to attack men of little importance when others who were greater had laid themselves open to attack.   Nor can it be said that Marat slurred anyone for the sheer joy he took in billingsgate.   He once claimed that he went to great pains to verify his charges.   Mistakes would occur, however, and needless to say, many of his denunciations were groundless and unnecessarily bitter. But on several occasions he apologized when he found he had been in the wrong; and once, at a time two years removed from the period we are now discussing, when he learned that an attack which he had directed against the Minister Roland was unjustified, he claimed to have destroyed the entire edition in which the charges were contained. Even in this magnanimity to his enemies, it is easy to appreciate his motives. It may have been nothing more than a sense of fairness that prompted him. Yet, how like a saintly and persecuted martyr he must have felt as he turned his other cheek to those who had already smitten him on the right, forgetting that he had himself been guilty of much hard smiting. Perhaps he reflected that even in martyrdom there was room to nourish an *amour de la gloire*.

*   *   *   *   *   *   *   *

If all the other idols of Marat had proved to have feet of clay and had collapsed under the first test, it was not so with Louis XVI. The King was eventually to go the way of Marat's other early heroes, but the love and respect that he had once had for Louis were not easily stifled. The confidence that the Friend of the People had placed in the King at the very beginning of the Revolution endured for some time to come. On October 6, 1789, when "the Baker, the Baker's wife, and the Baker's boy" were forced to return from Versailles to Paris with the women and the National Guard of the city, Marat shared the general feeling that somehow or other "his presence would soon change the face of things." Even amidst his bitter denunciations of Necker, he found words of praise for "the tender cares, the generous sacrifices of the monarch to provide subsistence for his people." As he watched the efforts of the Ministry and the aristocratic faction in the National Assembly to increase the authority of the King, he refused to believe that Louis was in league with them. "The King means well," he said. "Who does not know that? But his ministers mean only evil." And this attitude toward Louis continued for some months thereafter. In August 1790, in a pamphlet whose title would sound ludicrous if it were not so seriously meant (*On nous endort, Prenons-y garde*), he waxes almost enthusiastic:

> He is precisely the man we need. Without schemes, without artifice, without cunning, without craft, and hardly formidable to political liberty, he would be a good prince if he had enough tact to choose wise ministers.

Finally, toward the end of August 1790, he pronounced his last eulogy of Louis, on the occasion of the King's granting permission to the National Assembly to legislate upon certain of his own privileges. No one, Marat then declared, could realize the difficulties of the King's position better than he or appreciate the King's natural goodness more in acting so splendidly under strange and trying circumstances.

But indications were not lacking, even in the interim between the first of these pæans and the last, to make it manifest that Marat's affections for the King had been undergoing a gradual change. In spite of his good-will toward Louis XVI, his distrust of kings in general recurred intermittently. He was still intent upon restricting the monarch's power. That the king was but the first minister of the nation, that he derived his just powers from the consent of the nation, that he might even be subject to impeachment, that kings and especially royal ministers were with few exceptions inevitably corrupt and required careful surveillance, that they were equal in the eyes of the law to the lowest citizens—all these were tenets of his theory of state that he repeatedly expounded in the *Ami du Peuple*, often in the very issues in which he extolled Louis XVI. At this time, feeling that one journal did not provide a sufficient medium for his views, he contributed several articles to the paper of his disciple Fréron, editor of the *Orateur du Peuple*, and occasionally was responsible for entire numbers of that sheet.   But since that, too, seemed to him to be inadequate, on June 2, 1790, he began a second newspaper, which he called the *Junius Français*.   "I am going to fight for my country with two hands," he announced. But the effort proved to be too much even for his extraordinary ability to labor.   On June 24, after thirteen issues, it came to a close.   Anyone who had hoped that the new paper would follow a new policy was doomed to disappointment. Not only were the opinions of the *Junius Français* like those of the *Ami du Peuple*, but in the first numbers at least they were expressed in almost identical words.   It was clear from the numbers of the *Junius Français*, as well as from all the other writings of Marat at this period, that his fear of monarchy was struggling with his loyalty toward Louis XVI. Toward the end of July 1790 Marat republished his *Plan de législation criminelle* and in August presented a copy of it to the National Assembly.   With its numerous liberal contentions, this work accorded well with his changing attitude toward the King.   In short, he was becoming more and more confirmed in his old belief that royalty constantly arrogated to itself more than was its natural due, that kings were always and inevitably secretly engaged in manufacturing "chains of slavery," and that precautions must therefore be taken to check them.

In view of this feeling, it was only a matter of time until Marat should grow suspicious of Louis.   Consequently, when he witnessed the King's delay in sanctioning some of the decrees of the National Assembly, such as the radical measures acclaimed on August 4–5 and the vague aphorisms of the Declaration of the Rights of Man, his faith wavered.   He began to believe that the King himself was planning a counter-revolution, that he was seeking to flee from France, that he was attempting to gain control of the army, that he was in sympathy with the Count of Artois and others who were seeking alliances with foreign powers in order to destroy the Revolution. As he beheld the dread disease of counterrevolution infecting even the healthiest patriots, the only remedies he knew how to prescribe were warnings and accusations. On July 14, 1790, while France joyously celebrated the ceremony of the Federations on the Champ de Mars in honor of the first anniversary of the Fall of the Bastille, Marat denounced *The Damnable Scheme of the Enemies of the Revolution.* In an editorial by that title he declared that hordes of traitors would now be kept in influential positions by means of the civil list of twenty-five millions that had just been voted the King by an untrustworthy National Assembly. The police, who had rested from their pursuit of him since he had left for England in the preceding January, now replied by again raiding his printer's shop; and again Marat went into hiding. From his place of concealment he spread abroad further warnings. On July 26 came his famous tirade with the ominous title *C'en est fait de nous!* (*It Is All Up With Us!*) This was aimed at the émigrés—at those nobles and clerics who for the last year had been leaving France in continuous streams for the countries on the border, where, safe from the Revolution and its destruction, they might attack its works and urge apprehensive foreign princes to lead their armed forces against it. Many of these émigrés had gone to Coblenz, where the Count of Artois, the King's younger brother and quondam patron of Marat had set up court. The Queen was suspected of being in correspondence with them, with her brother, Leopold of Austria, and with other rulers of Europe, intending to restore the former royal status of the Bourbons by the aid of foreign armies if necessary. Recently one of her couriers had been arrested and, when Marat learned of the captive's mission, he beheld counter-revolution triumphant. It is all up with us, he cried. The émigrés, Savoy, Austria, the King, the Queen, the Princes—all are in conspiracy to destroy us and no one save the Friend of the People makes any efforts to protect us. "Five or six hundred heads cut off would have assured you peace, liberty and happiness. A false humanity has restrained your hand and delayed your blows. It is going to cost the lives of millions of your brothers."

This time not the Châtelet nor the Paris Commune but the National Assembly itself felt called upon to take action against the author. Through the initiative of Malouet, who had chanced to read Marat's pamphlet and had been stirred by its acrimony, a law was passed on July 31 declaring all writers, printers, and sellers of violent and seditious literature guilty of *lèse-nation*. On August 2 this was amended so as to have no retroactive effect save in the case of the leaflet entitled *C'en est fait de nous!* Consequently Marat was again forced into a month's seclusion. He had not been alone in attacking the suspicious activities of the court party, but his language had been by far the most ferocious and unrestrained. On August 2—of all days!—Marat chose to present to the National Assembly the new (third) edition of his *Plan de législation criminelle*. The minutes of the National Assembly record simply that the book was submitted—that is all. The Assembly on that day had more to say upon Marat the criminal than on Marat the criminologist. Despite its decrees, however, having already become expert in the art of not being on hand when the police most wanted him, Marat could not be apprehended and his journal continued to appear. On August 9 he warned the people against entertaining any sense of security. His pamphlet took the colorful title of *They Are Lulling Us to Sleep, Take Care* (*On nous endort, Prenons-y garde!*) in which, as we have already seen, he clung to his faith in Louis XVI, although he dreaded the evil effects of some of the palliative measures that had just been taken. Shortly afterwards came another cry to arouse the people to the fact that despite the calm in which the National Assembly was then carrying on its work, there was a storm abrewing— *C'est un beau rêve, Gare au Reveil!* (*It Is a Beautiful Dream, Watch out for the Awakening!*)

The impending storm broke when there came to Paris definite reports of what had happened in the so-called Nancy Affair. The garrison stationed at Nancy had caught the revolutionary fever which pervaded the French army after the Fête of the Federations celebrated at Paris on July 14, 1790. As a result it had become insubordinate and mutinous. General Malseigné, sent by the National Assembly to quell the rebellion, had been tactless and unsuccessful in his attempt to restore order and was himself maltreated. Finally General Bouillé, in command of the Army of the East, with some regular troops and National Guards attacked the Nancy garrison and forced it to surrender. Severe penalties were meted out to those involved in the mutiny.

From the very beginning of the affair Marat had been in sympathy with the undisciplined soldiers. In No. 10 of the *Junius Français* (June 13, 1790) he had given the news of a tumult at Nancy, where even thus early there seems to have been disorder and lack of discipline. Naturally he took the side of the soldiers against the officers. On August 18 he first mentioned the more recent events that had taken place at Nancy and reproached the Assembly for its unfriendly attitude toward the soldiers. In several subsequent issues he repeated these condemnations. Finally, on August 30 there appeared a pamphlet entitled *L'Affreux Reveil*, in which he placed the blame for the entire episode squarely upon the military and governmental officials. The Nancy Affair was for him plainly a victory of reactionary generals over patriotic soldiers. Here was the frightful awakening of which he had warned the dreamers lulled to sleep by the treacherous song of the counter-revolutionaries. His issues of September 1 and September 4 were devoted to attacks upon the officers of the Nancy garrison and chiefly upon General Bouillé. On September 12 he published a *Relation fidèle des malheureuses affaires de Nancy*, followed on September 18 by a *Relation authentique de ce qui s'est passé à Nancy*, both intended to shift the ill-will of the people, who had been terrified by the incipient revolt, from the unfortunate troops to their unworthy conquerors. In each he denounced the traitorous King and National Assembly for having given special thanks to Bouillé for putting down the mutiny. These pamphlets were but a few of the many arraignments that filled the regular issues of the *Ami du Peuple*, several of which exceeded and sometimes more than doubled the usual eight pages that Marat devoted to his journal.

It was therefore conspicuously true that the Nancy Affair had produced a tremendous effect upon Marat. He saw in it the beginning of the counter-revolutionary wave that he had long been anticipating. At first he laid the guilt directly upon the scheming ministers, although he regarded with suspicion "the attitude of wounded grief" which the King assumed. But when Louis praised Bouillé for his part in subduing the Nancy insurrection, Marat declared that the King was, in his mind, as much responsible for "the blood of the unfortunate patriots of Nancy" as the ministers and their supporters in the Assembly. It was "a frightful picture," he continued, for which, as long as he lived he would hold them all equally reprehensible. Again his agitation led him to set forth his theory of the subordinate position of the King: Louis XVI might be reduced to the rank of an ordinary citizen if the sovereign people so willed. But he did not yet indicate that he felt that the sovereign people ought so to will.

In May 1790 his fear that the monarch would take strenu-

ous measures to circumvent the Revolution grew stronger.   It
was about this time that the Spanish fleet drove some English
nationals out of Nootka Sound.   Pitt, the fiery English
Prime Minister, maintaining that Vancouver and the surrounding waters were English domain, immediately demanded
satisfaction from Spain.   For an anxious period it looked as
if there might be war between the bitterest enemy and the
staunchest friend of France.   In that case France would be
involved, for, by an alliance known as the Family Compact,
the Bourbons of France would be expected to go to the aid of
the Bourbons of Spain.   Mirabeau hoped to induce all parties
concerned to revoke the Family Compact and to substitute for
it a national alliance, but failed.   He did, however, succeed
in persuading the National Assembly to grant the King important powers in the conduct of diplomatic negotiations and
of war.   Marat had been seized with trembling lest Louis
should invoke the Family Compact, so that France would feel
called upon to go to the aid of her southern ally.   If that
came to pass, he expected the King to be clothed with dictatorial authority and thereby enabled to regain his original control over the country.   Fortunately, the Nootka Sound affair
passed almost as suddenly as it had begun, and the international atmosphere cleared.   But Marat continued to fret
about the internal effects of the tempest.   In the diplomatic
powers conferred upon the king he beheld a hidden instrument by which Louis would again attain a position of absolutism.   To prevent such a catastrophe, he urged the imprisonment of the royal family, the ministers, Lafayette and
Bailly, protesting that they were already directly involved
in treasonable relations with foreign powers.

While Marat was thus aroused by the Nancy and Nootka
Sound affairs, another incident occurred which served to increase his wrath.   In September 1790, a royalist demonstration took place in the town of Belfort, Alsace.   The event

was in itself entirely unimportant and passed almost un-
noticed by other journalists.   But Marat, never endowed with
a sense of proportion at any time, had already passed the stage
where he could distinguish between the trivial and the significant.   Anything now that bore the aspect of royalism
meant conspiracy and counter-revolution to him.   The Belfort episode, coming as it did while the horror of the Nancy
Affair was still fresh in his mind, evoked utterances that he
otherwise would have hesitated to express.

> The National Assembly [he cried] could dismiss the King and
> abolish the crown without causing the slightest commotion in the
> state. . . . It is a gross error to believe that the French govern-
> ment can no longer be anything but monarchical, that it even
> needs to be so to-day.

While he still held "that virtue upon the throne is the noblest
of the works of the Creator and, next to the immortal Author
of Nature . . . most worthy of worship," he had ceased to
believe that Louis possessed the necessary virtue.

It would seem, therefore, that although he had lost confidence in Louis XVI, he still clung to monarchy as a good form
of government.   But four days later (November 8, 1790),
he pronounced another anti-monarchical doctrine: "Every
prince born upon the throne is the dastardly enemy of the
people," or in other words, hereditary monarchy is necessarily
and inherently evil.   Applying this generalization to France,
he claimed that "for a man without prejudice, the King of the
French is worse than a fifth wheel to a cart, since he can only
put the political machine out of order."   After another interval of four days, he urged the coming legislature to strip the
monarch of almost all his power, or "what would be infinitely
better yet, to arrange the government after such a fashion that
the crown . . . would be proscribed."   The government that
he would have substituted for the one that existed was a sort

of a council greatly resembling the future Directory that ruled France from 1795 to 1799, with all administrative powers concentrated in the hands of an executive board of ministers.

For the moment, then, Marat had ceased to be a monarchist. The words *republic* and *republican* are hardly to be found in his writings up to this point, but the force of circumstances seemed to be leading him toward a staunch republicanism. At this time, too, the Civil Constitution of the Clergy placed Louis in a still more unfortunate light. It was a plan for the complete reorganization of the Gallican Church, making of the priesthood civil employees elected by the lay citizens, paid by the state, and divorced as nearly as possible from the control of Rome. All the Catholic and Bourbon scruples of Louis XVI revolted against it, and though it had passed the National Assembly and was supported by a clamorous element of the people, he refused to sanction it. Louis' hesitancy to consent to this sweeping reform revealed him to Marat as "the chief of the conspirators against the country." Within a brief period the People's Friend had even worked himself into a state of mind where he believed that he had "always regarded Louis XVI as the most deadly enemy of the Revolution."

While his conviction of the King's treachery was thus strengthening itself day by day, the older spectre of the flight of the royal family returned to haunt him. As a matter of fact, there had been more than one plot to kidnap the King and take him from Paris to more friendly regions of France, from which he might negotiate with the Assembly or, if necessary, dismiss it. Marat himself suspected Lafayette of complicity in these conspiracies, although he might with greater justice have directed his venom against the King's brother, the Count of Provence, and Mirabeau. The escape of the King, Marat feared, would form part of a larger scheme to desert France and to surrender Paris to her enemies for utter annihilation. It was inevitable and only natural, he thought, that a king and his agents, suddenly deprived of their power, should spend the rest of their days in planning to retrieve their fortunes. Almost reluctantly, it seems, he had persuaded himself that the King, his friends, his relatives, and his advisers were a sinister cabal and France was not safe as long as she was intrusted to his care.

The logical conclusion of all these contentions would have been for Marat to stand forth boldly in favor of the establishment of a republic. Certainly if courage had been all that was necessary, he would not have been found lacking. He had already suffered much for taking a stand that others regarded as dangerous and was still to suffer more. But he was not yet ready for such a step. As we shall see, he did not believe the republican form of government suitable for France, and while distrusting the monarchy, professed no greater confidence in the common people. Despite his previous anti-monarchical avowals, a temporary return to his old belief in monarchy was therefore inevitable. It came rather suddenly on February 17, 1791. In the issue of his paper on that date, Marat declared:

> I do not know whether the counter-revolution will force us to change our form of government, but I do know that *very limited monarchy* is what fits us best to-day, in view of the depravity and baseness of the supporters of the ancient regime, all so much disposed to abuse the powers that have been confided to them. With such men a federated republic would soon degenerate into oligarchy.

Marat's eighteenth century philosophical background did not make it possible for him to conceive of all France as a single republic, and almost any kind of monarchy seemed more tolerable than a federated republic. As for the King, he went on, he still considered him "made of excellent stuff" with but the defects of his education:

All things considered, he is the King we need. We ought to thank heaven for having given him to us. We ought to pray to it to preserve him for us.

But despite this declaration, his opposition to Louis continued. He beheld the shadow of the counter-revolution lurking everywhere. The horror of the conspiracy of the Queen and the Count of Artois with foreign powers especially fascinated him. He was inclined to believe that the King, if not the leader of the conspirators, was at least their rallying-point. Besides, he became constantly more and more convinced of the King's intention to take flight. For a few months in 1791, until the King actually did attempt to leave France, Marat kept urging almost daily that measures be taken to prevent such a contingency. He feared that even if Louis did not take the step of his own accord, he might be abducted by those whose interest it was to present a strong front against the Revolution. On April 18, the royal family did make an effort to leave the Tuileries for St. Cloud, but it was halted by a hostile demonstration. Marat was elated, but insisted that now even greater vigilance was necessary than ever before. He was again led into extravagant declarations. At this moment his animus was undoubtedly directed only against Louis personally and not against monarchy as an institution. Yet he now announced that he regarded as tools and hirelings of the King all those who preached that a state such as France must be a monarchy, forgetting that but two months before he had himself expressed that very thought.

Marat had good reason to rejoice that the royal family had been prevented from leaving the Tuileries on April 18, for they actually were planning, even at that early date, to escape from France in order to join the émigrés and foreign rulers waiting to march into Paris and overwhelm the Revolution. The death of Mirabeau on April 2 had deprived the King of a sagacious, though distrusted adviser, who had been willing to consent to flight only on condition that it would lead to no complications with foreign powers. Now that his restraining influence was removed, the Queen became more and more insistent upon leaving France, with the intention of returning at the head of a foreign force which would suppress the miserable Revolution. The failure of the attempt on April 18 merely caused the royal family to appreciate the necessity for future preparations. Finally on June 21, 1791, Louis justified Marat's worst fears by actually escaping, in disguise, with his family, leaving behind a declaration in which he repudiated all the work of the National Assembly and the Revolution.

We shall leave for consideration in another chapter the revolutionary measures that the Friend of the People now proposed. Suffice it here to say that he showed the same consternation that on the whole pervaded all of Paris through fear that the King might make good his escape and return with a hostile army. Fortunately the royal family were arrested near the border of France and brought back to Paris. Upon the enforced return of the monarch, the National Assembly sought to make it appear that Louis had not been a free moral agent in his flight, but had been abducted against his own will. Marat, however, shared the views of the more radical of the Jacobins and the Cordeliers, and instituted a series of demands for the trial, imprisonment and even execution of the King for treason. On one occasion he stated that the people of France desired the abolition of royalty altogether, but he himself would have been satisfied with a regency, though not of the Capetian house (by which he meant the Duke of Orleans) until the Dauphin came of age. He suggested Robespierre as the one most fit to educate the Dauphin properly in the meantime.

The Cordeliers and part of the Jacobins proposed petitions for the deposition of the King. They were drawn up and put

upon a table in the Champ de Mars for those who favored
them to sign. On July 17, 1791 two unfortunates were found
hiding under the table. They were suspected of being government spies and lynched. To preserve order, Bailly and
Lafayette, as Mayor and Commander-in-Chief of the National
Guard of Paris, read the riot act—a decree of martial law
against which Marat had vigorously protested ever since it
had become law on October 21, 1789. The crowd refused to
disperse and the National Guard fired. The mob fled, leaving several of its number dead and dying behind them.
Though Marat's attitude toward the captive ruler had been
essentially like that of the sponsors of the petitions that had
resulted in the so-called Massacre of the Champ de Mars,
there is no evidence that he had any direct connection with
that unhappy incident. But so outraged was he by the murderous assault of the National Guard upon unarmed citizens
that he defied the National Assembly, which he held responsible for the disaster, in violent tones that furnish an apposite
example of his invective in its most trenchant form:

> As for the Friend of the People, you have long known that all of
> your decrees opposed to the Rights of Man are only *torche-culs*
> for him. Would that he could rally to his voice two thousand de-
> termined men! To save the country he would go at their head to
> tear out the heart of the infernal Mottier [Lafayette] in the midst
> of his battalion of slaves. He would go to burn the monarch and
> his henchmen in his palace. He would go to impale you upon
> your seats and bury you under the flaming débris of your lair.

As a result of this harangue, there was another raid made
upon the *Ami du Peuple*. Madamoiselle Colombe, his printer,
was arrested and imprisoned; the entire edition containing
the attack upon the National Assembly was seized and the
plates destroyed. But, as usual, Marat himself was nowhere
to be found. His place of concealment in these times of
crisis was generally the cellar of the Convent of the Cordeliers

or the home of some friend, and not, as is generally supposed, the sewers of Paris; and it was probably the cellar of the Convent of the Cordeliers, not far from where he then made his home, to which he now went for shelter.   So closely, however, did he have to keep hidden that his journal ceased to appear regularly for the first time since his return from England in April 1790.   Between July 21 and August 10, 1791, only one number was published.

Much to the undisguised displeasure of Marat, Louis XVI was restored to his throne upon the acceptance of the new Constitution of 1791.   Thus, in September 1791, France became a constitutional monarchy.   Even under the new regime, Marat's feeling that the King was still in conspiracy against the Revolution and would again attempt flight would not down, and he urged the populace to surround the Assembly, demanding action against the émigrés and the suspension of the King.   Although the details of Marat's career for the next few months can best be discussed in connection with his attitude toward the Constitution of 1791, it should be pointed out here that his hostility toward Louis continued undiminished until the end of 1791, when Marat, for reasons that will appear later, found it advisable to withdraw again to England for several months, and, indeed, until Louis' death.

While Marat thus beheld the individuals in whom he had at first placed his confidence—Lafayette, Necker, the King—failing him everywhere, his hope in the successful completion of an acceptable constitution for France dwindled *pari passu* away.   He had rejoiced with the rest of France when feudalism was mitigated in the memorable epidemic of enthusiasm that seized the deputies of the National Assembly on August 4 and 5, 1789.   But he did not feel that the nobility who had hectically surrendered their privileges and dues one after the other on that glorious occasion deserved the gratitude that a thankful country poured forth: the surrender had not been made out of sheer good-will and patriotism, but only at the sight of peasants with arms in their hands setting flames to the lords' chateaux and demanding the amelioration of their lot.   The Declaration of the Rights of Man he greeted with approval, having constantly insisted that the rights of the people must first be established before the privileges of the king were determined.   How he declaimed against Mounier's proposal of a bicameral legislature and an absolute veto for the king we have already seen.   He had also opposed the granting even of a suspensive veto to the king, which had been passed by the National Assembly and incorporated in the proposals of the Second Committee on the Constitution. Nevertheless, for a short time following this decree, he adopted as attitude of approbation toward the work of the Second Committee.   Yet some suggestions which were being made for the reorganization of the French government moved him to an outburst of angry protest.   While he favored the restriction of the number of delegates to the national legislature, he took exception to the method of limiting them by a property qualification.   He therefore opposed the decree of the *marc d'argent*, which fixed the property qualifications of deputies at a contribution in direct taxes of a silver mark (about fifty livres), on the grounds that it made possible the election of only rich men and nobles, excluding a large number of poorer men who might be better fitted for membership in the country's law-making body.   For much the same reason he objected to the division of France into active and passive citizens.   Marat, who had always insisted that birth alone entitled a man to the right to vote, could naturally have no sympathy with a decree which gave the privilege of suffrage only to those whose direct contribution in taxes amounted to three days' wages.   By such a measure the mass of the working people (about a third of the adult males of France), who were to his mind the best citizens of the country, were deprived of all influence upon the political fortunes of the state. He declared the act null and void because it violated the Declaration of the Rights of Man, which had declared all men equal, and enjoined the people to disregard it.   He had dreaded that the effect of such a law would be to force the poorer citizens to emigrate from France, and when he heard of fifty workers leaving Paris for Worms, he felt that his fears had been well founded.

Another law that convinced him of the utter corruption of the National Assembly was the decree rendering deputies inviolable and declaring that they represented, not the community from which they were sent, but the nation at large.   He looked for this decree to make the representatives independent of their constituencies and called for resistance by all true patriots.   To declare the members of the Assembly inviolable struck him as tantamount to giving to scoundrels in the legislature the right to conspire with impunity against their fellow-countrymen and delivering up Paris especially to their mercy. Furthermore, in Marat's political philosophy, the *sine qua non* of any constitution was its acceptance by the people.   To make the representatives independent of their constituencies was to render possible a constitution that would be entirely unsatisfactory to the French nation.   He had already, on frequent occasions, presented one of his favorite theories: that the honest citizen owed no obedience to unjust laws.   Not that Marat was wittingly an anarchist, as he has so often been charged with being, for he himself denied that charge; but he did believe, as apologists for revolution have always believed, that governments, to be obeyed, must be righteous.   Now that he was afraid that the National Assembly was endeavoring to make itself independent of the people, he refused to consider the constitution as effective until it had met with the approval of the people in a popular referendum.

Several measures on military affairs which emanated from

the National Assembly also angered him.   Marat was to a
large extent a pacifist and opposed to the army except as an
instrument under the control of the people.   The decree of
October 21, 1789 that regulated the declaration of martial
law filled him with apprehension: it left too much to the dis-
cretion and intelligence of military officers, who were notori-
ously indiscreet and unintelligent, and surrendered Paris and
other French communities to their good will; and he had very
little confidence even in their good will.   Mirabeau, he announced, would ever be anathema because of his support of
this measure, and Robespierre ever blessed because of his opposition to it.   It was all a part of a grand conspiracy to put
complete military power in the hands of the king.   So, too,
were the decrees affecting the National Guard.   Marat wished
the National Guard to be composed of all citizens, passive as
well as active, who should be allowed to use their own discre-
tion in obeying the commands of their officers.   Within the
ranks of the National Guard there were to be no distinctions
of prestige between infantry, dragoons, or grenadiers; and all
officers were to be elected by the vote of the troops.   In the
Nancy Affair Marat saw the natural consequences of the general notion that soldiers must be unquestioningly obedient to
the orders of their superior officers.   Therefore when the National Assembly took under consideration the re-organization
of the National Guard (September 1790–April 1791) and
finally decreed that it was to be open only to active citizens
and was a force "essentially obedient," Marat's indignation
mounted to a high pitch.   He saw three million citizens who
"had taken up arms only to destroy despotism" deprived of
all the benefits of the new era of democracy and "metamor-
phosed into henchmen of despotism."   Only a few of the
richer (and therefore less desirable) citizens could join it,
while the mass of the most patriotic were excluded.   Soon he
expected to see the newly organized National Guard led

against their countrymen and kinsfolk unquestioningly, even willingly.

The last and crowning act in the militaristic cabal was its attempt to put into the hands of the king the right to declare war and peace. This matter was taken up by the National Assembly in May 1790, at a time when France was faced by the grave possibility of war with England. As already pointed out, Spain, her ally by the Family Compact, was in heated controversy with England regarding their respective rights in Nootka Sound. Marat was intent upon keeping peace with England, in whose people he at this time saw a friend of the French Revolution. Furthermore, he knew France to be entirely unprepared for the emergency and feared that a war at the present juncture would, as indeed many royalists hoped, concentrate military power in the hands of the King and enable him to destroy the Revolution. Even when he thought he saw in certain of the demands of the English ambassador a deliberate attempt to provoke hostilities, he advised compliance in order to preserve amicable relations. In the midst of such a diplomatic crisis Marat was particularly anxious to avoid putting the right to declare war in the hands of a Bourbon, in honor bound to respect the *Pacte de Famille*. The National Assembly had divided into two parties on the question: one that upheld the king's right both to declare and to prosecute war, and the other that was willing to leave him the right to prosecute war, but maintained that peace could be broken only with the consent of the national legislature. Marat, of course, favored the second party. The decree which was finally enacted embodied this plan in large part, but it also included several provisions to which Marat was opposed. He maintained, for example, that it did not repudiate the Family Compact, to which he objected as an alliance with an autocratic nation; it gave the king too much influence in the making of treaties; it put him in a position to manipulate the national troops for his own benefit. Besides, he did not think that the King would adhere to the provisions of the decree. The entire measure, therefore, was merely an effort to involve France in future conflicts for the ulterior interests of the royalists. Finally, in August 1790, when Mirabeau proposed the re-organization of the national troops, Marat objected on the grounds that a new army would become the instrument of tyranny. He even objected to inserting the King by name or title in the new oath of allegiance required of the country's soldiers. The truth was that the King had now been deprived of many of his powers in conducting military and foreign affairs, which formerly had been practically absolute. Marat, however, had eyes only for those that still remained, and in them he saw a sufficient means for Louis to involve the country in war for trivial causes and thereby regain his former position of autocracy.

In addition to these political and military measures there were several financial enactments for which Marat also condemned the National Assembly. The financial debacle of the Ancient Regime had been the immediate cause of the convocation of the Estates General and therefore of the Revolution. The National Assembly had tried several palliative measures that had failed. Finally it decided to confiscate the property of the Gallican Church, which was valued at more than enough to pay off the portion of the national debt that was soluble. With this property as security it issued five per cent bonds known as *assignats* to the debtors of the state. After a short while the interest on the *assignats* was abolished and they began to circulate as paper money. Marat had, at the very beginning of the debates upon the issue of *assignats*, pointed out that their effect would be to waste the government goods, concentrating them in the hands of a few speculators and leaving the poor as miserable as ever. Subsequent developments proved his foresight to have been only too accurate.

The *assignats* depreciated as more and more of them were printed, as counterfeiting increased, and as the land-value which they represented was lowered. They soon began to circulate at less than face value. Marat in the meantime insisted that economy was more reliable as a fiscal remedy. The enormous expenditures for naval and military purposes, he declared, had been the cause of the dilapidation of the nation's finances and he demanded severe retrenchment now. He urged, too, that pensions and allowances granted to relatives of the king and members of the Academy and other honorary societies should be curtailed or entirely abolished. He was indignant when he learned that while the National Assembly had appropriated millions for these purposes, it believed itself able to vote only 30,000 livres for distribution among eight or ten thousand survivors of a recent flood in the valleys of the Loire and the Rhone.

Such, then, was his attitude toward the new constitutional legislation. Certain acts of the National Assembly of a political nature, though in no way connected with formation of the new constitution, likewise drew upon that body his acrimonious reproaches. Chief among these were the approbation of Bouillé's conduct in relation to the Nancy Affair and the delay in agreeing to the annexation of Avignon, a papal dominion entirely surrounded by France and now seeking admission into the French nation. Bouillé's ruthlessness in suppressing the mutiny of the Chateauvieu regiment during the Nancy Affair, we already know, met with Marat's severest condemnation, and the approval and thanks that the National Assembly gave him were for Marat but another indication of its aristocratic tendencies. The annexation of Avignon presented several practical difficulties. There was first the necessity of assurance that the will of the people of Avignon and not simply a Gallophile minority was in favor of such an annexation. There was secondly the fear that in appropri-

ating the property of the Pope, international complications
with which the National Assembly was in no position to cope
might arise. But to Marat it was a simple question of pro-
moting the cause of democracy and therefore the Assembly's
delay meant nothing to him but its lack of democratic principles. These and many other measures of the National Assembly encountered an indignant and furious opposition from
Marat. In all of them his suspicious nature caused him to
discern a carefully laid counter-revolutionary plot.

While it is true that the National Assembly was largely
inspired by bourgeois interests and preconceptions, Marat was
entirely wrong in attributing to it a conscious and deliberate
conspiracy to reëstablish the absolutism of the Ancient Regime. In his failure to perceive this, he had lost faith in the
National Assembly completely. None of its leaders—Bailly,
Lafayette, Mirabeau, Barnave—appeared to him to be pure
democrats and patriots. Only Robespierre and one or two
other comparatively obscure deputies held any place in his
regard. All the rest were tools of the court, devoid of all
conception of patriotism, scheming only to restore, measure
by measure, the former power of the king. He believed that
they had even corrupted the patriotic clubs. What rankled
especially was their failure to enact his measures to prevent
the king from exercising too great a control over legislation.
He repeated again and again that with such men as leaders,
France was doomed and could never hope to be free. His
whole policy with regard to the National Assembly presents
another instance of his inability properly to evaluate the motives of those who disagreed with him and his inclination to
pity himself as a righteous martyr.

When the constitution drawn up by this organization of
"traitors" was nearing the point of completion, Marat discovered that in addition to its many sins of commission, it was
culpable of even grosser sins of omission. The National As-

sembly had failed to put the strings of the nation's purse in the hands of the legislature, and he feared that the king would become the controller of the government's finances. Actually, however, this was a groundless fear, since the king had no right to appropriate taxes or raise revenue in any way without the consent of the legislature.   Furthermore, Marat looked askance at the new constitution because it had not established a supreme court and its interpretation was left a constant source of strife.   Finally, to say nothing of various minor omissions, no provision had been made for the enforcement of the Declaration of the Rights of Man.   Since the National Assembly had omitted to create an adequate machinery for amending the constitution, Marat contended that the coming Legislative Assembly ought to be empowered to revise it completely.

A sorry constitution indeed it was in Marat's opinion and he did not hesitate to air his grievances.   Time and again he pronounced it a complete failure.   He had objected to the oath of fidelity to the constitution required at the Federations of July 14, 1790.   He now desired to see future legislatures annul it entirely with the exception of the Declaration of Rights.   As early as June 1790 he had expounded the power for evil which was being entrusted to the King.   Now that the work of the National Assembly was over, he claimed that the only result of the Revolution had been to render the king more absolute than he had ever been by destroying the nobility and the *parlements*, which had hitherto been the sole obstacles in the way of absolute despotism.   The whole state of affairs seemed to him to be worse than it had been in the Ancient Regime.   Money had disappeared; prices had gone up; food was scarce; unemployment was general; taxes were heavy; justice was difficult to obtain; civil war was inevitable.

Back in April 1791 Marat had begun to consider the advisability of leaving France for England.   But months passed before he could bring himself to the point of abandoning his adopted country.   In September he was plainly disheartened and definitely decided to go again to England, which he had once called "the only country in the world that a wise man would choose as an asylum."   On September 8 he announced to his readers his intention of giving up his journalistic enterprises.   But he surrendered his editorial pen only with the greatest reluctance.   On September 12, he administered a parting thrust at the Academy in a volume entitled *Le Charlatanisme académique*.   In this book he arraigned, with no more emphasis however than upon other Academicians, the chemist Lavoisier, not only for what he considered a lack of real scientific attainment, but also because Lavoisier had been a farmergeneral of taxes under the old regime and was suspected of being opposed to the Parisian populace.   On account of this attack Marat has frequently been accused of having caused Lavoisier's death by the guillotine.   But since Lavoisier was not executed until ten months after Marat's own death, it is hardly probable that Marat was directly responsible for the execution of the famous chemist, even if he was unable to understand Lavoisier's real scientific merit.

On September 21 Marat made his "final adieus" in a statement whose moderation, all the more surprising because of the fiery tone of the issues of the preceding few days, was a sort of admission of defeat.   Refusing to be included in the general amnesty that the National Assembly had magnanimously passed as its concluding act, he departed.   But even outside of Paris, he watched over his brood.   The issue of the *Ami du Peuple* for September 22 was dated from Clermont; the next from Breteuil; the next from Amiens.   His own story was that he found that police spies were on his trail (why they should have continued to hound him after the general amnesty, even though he had refused to accept its application to him, is not clear) and in order to avoid falling into their hands, he had made his way back to Paris, with some difficulty and only with the aid of a friendly shepherd, who helped him to hide. Perhaps he never really left Paris; perhaps if he did, his reason for returning was other than the story that he told. But at any rate on September 27 he was in Paris again or still. His paper had suffered only one day's lapse between the 21st and the 27th.

After his return, obliged to resign himself to circumstances for a time, he pinned his hopes to the coming Legislative Assembly. He may have felt that since the traitors of the National Assembly had magnanimously decreed themselves ineligible for the Legislative Assembly, there was room for expectation that the latter body might contain some honest patriots. He had himself been suggested as a candidate for this Assembly, but his name had appeared upon only one ballot and on that he had received only two votes out of a possible seven hundred and thirty-three. Evidently the friendship of the Friend of the People was not yet reciprocated by the people. On several occasions Marat had already expressed a hope that the Legislative Assembly would enact needed reforms. The first representatives to be elected had disappointed him, but after his attempted departure and subsequent return his expectations were once more revived. "If the coming legislature is not as rotten as the National Assembly," he none too optimistically declared, "it is possible that patriots will arise, that liberty will become firmly established."

His hopes were soon shattered. He wanted to see the Legislative Assembly devote itself to the consideration of the steps to be taken against the émigré nobility. The Assembly, however, consumed a large part of the first month of its existence in fruitless discussion of its organization and questions of etiquette in its relations with the court. This evident frivolity made Marat restless and destroyed his renewed faith. "The new Conscript Fathers," he decided very soon, "are no

better than the old." When decrees against the émigrés, requiring them to return before the New Year on pain of losing
their property if they failed to do so, finally were passed,
Marat found them wholly inadequate and thought that too
long a recess was provided until they became active. In December new grounds for hostility arose. He found the Assembly engaged in discussing the expediency of war with the
Empire and Prussia. Queen Marie Antoinette had kept constantly importuning her brother Leopold, the Emperor of the
Holy Roman Empire, for aid against her husband's revolutionary subjects. The émigrés and particularly the Count of
Artois, added their prayers to hers. The Emperor, moreover,
feared that revolutionary ideals might permeate his realms;
already the German princes who owned lands in Alsace had
complained to him because of the losses that the confiscation
of feudal dues inside of France had caused them. As soon as
Leopold learned of the failure of Louis XVI's attempt to
escape from France in June 1791, he issued the notorious document known as the Padua Circular urging the rulers of
Europe to unite against the "violent party" in France. Only
Prussia accepted. In August the two rulers stated in the
Declaration of Pillnitz that if the other sovereigns of Europe
joined them, they would use force on Louis's behalf. Leopold did not expect the other sovereigns to join him and therefore felt safe in issuing the Declaration, but France was
outraged. Louis XVI wanted war, feeling that defeat would
be assigned to the weakness of a democratic government and
victory to his own leadership. The Brissotins, the radical
faction of the Legislative Assembly, also wanted war in order
to overthrow tyrants, unite the French, and perhaps reveal the
treachery of the King. In December Louis thought to bring
about hostilities only with the Archbishop of Trèves, who
harbored the émigrés. But as the Emperor gave aid to the
Archbishop, Austria became involved and Prussia was in al-

liance with Austria.   War on a huge scale seemed inevitable.
To such a war, Marat, fearing the outcome, was heartily adverse.   Even before Austria had become thoroughly aroused,
he urged a more pacific policy.   His admonitions received no
attention, however, and in disgust with Frenchmen and the
Legislative Assembly in particular, he again prepared to leave
for England.   He now felt that the cause of the Revolution
was hopeless, and could see safety only in a general insurrection and guerilla warfare in case of invasion by a foreign
enemy.   On December 14 he bade farewell to his subscribers
and on the 15th was on his way to London.   This time he
reached his destination.

In England he set to work to provide what a cynical biographer might call still another example of the dictum that he
who knows not, teaches.   He devoted the period of his sojourn to writing an *École du citoyen*.   He himself assures
us that any sincere patriot could learn from it the correct
way to proceed on all important questions.   It was designed
"to put the people on their guard against unfaithful leaders,
to reveal the traps set by rascals bribed to ensnare them, to
make known what old laws needed reform and what new ones
were necessary in order to insure liberty and public happiness."   He returned to France late in February or early in
March 1792.   If he ever seriously intended to remain permanently in England, perhaps his belief that the French might
profit more from his *École du citoyen* than the English led
him to change his mind.   At any rate, the first indication we
have of his presence in Paris chances to be a letter to the
President of the Society of the Cordeliers in which he asks
the Society to help him circulate a prospectus of the book
among all the patriotic clubs of France.   Though the Cordeliers co-operated cordially with him in this adventure, the
book never was published and was found in manuscript among
his papers when an inventory of his possessions was made upon

his death. An attempt that he made to get government aid in publishing this and two other manuscripts got no further than the unfriendly Roland's office.

Upon his return to France, the paramount issue of the day still was the question of war against the émigrés, the Emperor, and Prussia. Marat was unable to bring his views on this subject before the people, for in the production of his journal he had exhausted whatever wealth he had been able to accumulate in the more affluent days before the Revolution and now had no means of continuing his publication. After a month of silence, during which he was urged by the Society of the Cordeliers to renew publication and was promised their unstinted support, he was able to issue the paper again with money furnished him by Simonne Evrard. The story of Simonne Evrard is the most romantic of all the amatory episodes in Marat's life. Except for the liaison with the Marquise de Laubespine it was perhaps the only serious affair of his career. For Marat was remarkably puritan for an intellectual of the eighteenth century. There probably is little or no truth, for example, in Madame Roland's story of the young lady who, seeking a favor for one of her friends, went to visit Marat and found a languishing sensualist in a luxurious apartment. Marat at no time during the Revolution could afford luxury of any description. The association of his name with the actress, Madame Fleury, rests on nothing more than the fact that, as we shall find, she was released from prison in 1794 as a reward for having once helped Marat to hide from the police. There were also a novice in a convent and a maltreated mistress whom he befriended, the latter not without protest from her lover and salacious comments from his political opponents, but these affairs are known to us chiefly through Marat's own accounts and therefore are reasonably free from any breath of scandal unfavorable to him. Of his relations with Angelica Kaufman, whom Marat knew in England, we know little save through the innuendoes, probably groundless, of Brissot's *Mémoires*.

But Simonne Evrard was his wife in all but name in the last year or so of his life.   He knew the Evrard family and had been befriended by it on several occasions of stress. Simonne Evrard was formally affianced to him and in December 1791 (though the document is dated as of the New Year of 1792), when he left for England, he set down in writing that is still extant his promise to marry her for the kindness she had shown him and the love he bore her.   The marriage ceremony when performed would probably not have received the sanction of any church or government of his day or this, but it was in complete accordance with Marat's Rousseauan philosophy.   Sometime in the early part of 1792 he took Simonne to wife "before the Supreme Being . . . in the vast temple of Nature."   There is no reason to believe that this was an act of libertinage.   Marat in his *Plan de législation criminelle* had had some harsh things to say of libertinage, and for his day, was rather a puritan.   Simonne Evrard and he seem to have lived fairly happily together until his assassination.   It was she to whom his last words—a call for help —were addressed.   After his death she was received by his family, who up to this time had remained indifferent not only to her existence but also to his, and was universally known as *la veuve Marat*.

It was with the aid of Simonne Evrard, then, that Marat resumed the *Ami du Peuple* on April 12, 1792.   In order to distinguish it as authentic from the alleged *Amis du Peuple*, of which he claimed there were no less than five that had come into existence in his absence, he prefixed to the first few numbers the letter from the Cordeliers in which he was requested to renew its publication.   He immediately adopted a stand of opposition to war, persisting in finding in it the last effort of the royalists to defeat the Revolution by concentrating war powers in the hands of the king. He regarded France as totally unprepared for the conflict, its generals incapable and ready to betray her, and disaffected elements willing to aid the enemy. His plan to prevent war was to hold Louis and his family as hostages, their lives being forfeit if the enemy invaded France. Needless to say, this proposal was not adopted, and the Legislative Assembly declared war upon the foes of France on April 20, 1792. Even after hostilities had begun, Marat believed that if his advice were followed, Louis' allies would not dare to continue their aggressions.

His inflammatory statements again came to the attention of the national representative body. We are informed by Prudhomme, a contemporary journalist, that, together with the Emperor and the *émigrés*, Marat was the chief source of the anxiety of the Legislative Assembly for a time. Finally on May 3, 1792, after a protracted debate, a decree of accusation was carried against him. This was done largely in order to appease Lafayette and other generals at the front, who were disgruntled by the radicalism of Paris and certain factions of the Assembly. Royou, editor of the *Ami du roi*, a royalist sheet, was likewise included in this decree. Again Marat took to his subterranean retreats, and strenuous measures were taken to capture him. About this time (May 18), the Legislative Assembly passed a law to the effect that every resident of Paris, under penalty of fine or imprisonment, must make known to the Committee of his Section every person living with him. The measure was probably a war measure, but perhaps Marat and his biographers have been right in thinking it had something to do with his own pursuit. Though his name was not associated with the debates on this particular decree, the failure of the police to reach him was twice called to the attention of the Legislative Assembly (May 21 and June 12) within the next few weeks. At any rate he kept more carefully hidden than usual. As frequently before, the

lapses in the appearance of the *Ami du Peuple* furnish us with
a rather accurate register of the degree of care he employed in
remaining concealed; and we now find that his journal, which
had appeared with surprising regularity since the preceding
April, was issued rarely between June 3 and June 15, ceased
entirely thereafter until July 7, and during the next month
was published only ten times.

While Marat thus kept closely confined to his place of
refuge in order to avoid arrest, events in France moved fast.
Hostilities against Austria had already begun and inefficiency,
corruption, and treachery in the army became evident, just as
Marat had foretold. The French attack upon the Austrian
Netherlands failed and the soldiers retreated in confusion, mas-
sacring their officers.   It was suspected with some reason that
Marie Antoinette had betrayed the French plans to the enemy.
To make matters worse, the King again refused to sanction
the decrees of the Legislative Assembly that were intended to
punish the émigrés and the clergy who would not accept the
Civil Constitution.   When the ministry disapproved of his
action, having like a true Bourbon learned nothing from the
results of the dismissal of Necker in July 1789, he now dismissed Roland and others of his most capable and most popular ministers.   In reply the people of Paris invaded the
Tuileries on June 20, 1792 and forced the King to wear the
revolutionary cap, although they could not make him yield on
the matter of the decrees or the ministers.   Reports of this
uprising came to the émigrés, Austrians, and Prussians preparing to invade France.   On July 25 Prussia declared war and
a few days later the Duke of Brunswick issued his famous
impolitic manifesto, threatening dire consequences to Paris if
the King suffered any further humiliation or harm.   Opposition to Louis, and with it the power of the republican spirit,
had been developing rapidly inside of France.   As was to be
expected, Paris, already in a frenzy of patriotism and anti-

royalism, prepared for another insurrection when it learned of the Brunswick Manifesto. On August 10 the Tuileries was again attacked. The ineffectual attempt of the Swiss Guard and loyal nobles to protect the King and his family resulted only in their massacre. Louis, who, with the Queen and the Dauphin, had taken refuge in the Legislative Assembly, was suspended from his office and imprisoned in the Temple. The French monarchy had fallen, and a National Convention was called to determine the will of the people in the reorganization of the state.

The insurrection of August 10, 1792, unlike the previous popular movements of the French Revolution, had been coolly premeditated by the leaders of the Paris proletariat. Marat, however, was not among them, for he had not dared to come forth openly from his place of hiding since May 3. Nevertheless, in the few issues of the *Ami du Peuple* that appeared between May 3 and August 10 he kept up his unending cry for action against the royal family. On August 9 he published a *Lettre de l'Ami du peuple aux Fédérés des Quatre-vingt-trois départements* summoning them to

> hold as hostages Louis XVI, his wife, his son, his ministers, all your unfaithful representatives, all the members of the old departments and the new, all the venal judges of the peace. These are the traitors of whom the nation ought to demand justice and whom it ought first to sacrifice to the public welfare.

Appeals such as this make it necessary to consider Marat responsible to a certain extent for the events of August 10, 1792. Exactly to what a degree he was responsible it would be difficult to discover, since there are no statistics available for the circulation of his paper nor any other means of determining his exact influence upon the Paris populace at this time. The historian Villiaumé, who claimed to have used Marat's own notes as a source for his statements on the Friend of the People in his *Histoire de la Révolution*, alleges that fifty thousand copies of the *Ami du Peuple* for August 19, nine days after the insurrection, were printed, but this figure must be taken solely on his authority and is open to grave doubt. Yet it may be stated on *a priori* grounds that the mob that attacked the Tuileries on August 10 was of the very class to whom the *Ami du Peuple* made its appeal and that therefore many of them had read and had been roused to action by his persistent demands for the imprisonment of the royal household.

Not until August 10 did Marat come out of hiding. His first act was to issue an address—*L'Ami du Peuple aux fran-çais patriotes*—in which he again argued that it was a treacherous policy that dictated mercy for counter-revolutionaries:

No quarter! You are irrevocably lost if you do not hasten to beat down the rotten members of the municipality and the department, all antipatriotic justices of the peace, and the most gangrened members of the national assembly. . . . No one more than I abhors the spilling of blood; but to prevent floods of it from flowing, I urge you to pour out a few drops.

He demanded again that the royal family and those in league with them be kept as hostages, their lives to be forfeit if the enemy did not withdraw from the territory of France. Although his advice was not taken, he did make one distinct gain through the events of August 10. The Committee of Police and Surveillance of the Paris Commune presented him with four of the royal presses, which were taken from the Louvre and set up in the cellar of the Convent of the Cordeliers. He did not steal them, as Michelet and others have contended. Now the *Ami du Peuple*, which had formerly depended for its existence upon a number of printers varying in ability and faithfulness, was issued independently and dependably from the *imprimerie de Marat*. Instead of being hunted from place to place, its editor now enjoyed official recognition.

As a result of the Tenth of August, the Legislative Assembly called for a new representative body which was to take the name of the National Convention and to establish the first French Republic. But as yet Marat was a monarchist. During the months of April to August 1792, the republican movement in France had grown from an aspiration entertained by a handful of idealists into a program soon to be accomplished. In this development, Marat, despite his opposition to Louis XVI personally, had had no part. So far was he from advocating an abolition of monarchy that in September 1791, when he made his trip to Amiens in his ineffectual attempt to leave France and had the occasion to be a fellow-traveller with some grumbling *ci-devants*, he had proposed that the titles and other innocuous honors of former nobles be returned to them for the sake of avoiding the trouble that they otherwise might create. To be sure, the very next month he did state that "as long as the crown is hereditary, the prince will be the eternal enemy of the nation and his ministers will always be rascals paid to execute his evil plans," but within another month, calling for a general insurrection to drive out the Capets, he urged that a new constitution be drawn up which, while based on the liberal program he had continually advocated, was to provide for a prince to whom was to be entrusted "the right of sending and receiving ambassadors, proposing treaties with foreign powers, and accepting the generals named by the army." Finally, on August 7, 1792, within little more than a month before the Republic was actually established in France, in commenting on the commotion caused by the Brunswick Manifesto, he asserted that all France was demanding the deposition of Louis XVI and the election of a new king; he said not a word about a republic. Even if we assume that this was merely a statement of fact and that his wish was not father to his thought, there is still the silence of Marat, who spoke neither for nor against this supposed demand of all France, to account for; and silence on the part of Marat, who rarely was silent on things to which he objected, was acquiescence indeed. If we are to infer anything at all from this statement, whether it be taken as fact or propaganda, it is that the most radical change Marat advocated at this time was merely a change in kings and not a change from kingship to republic.

The conclusion seems to be, therefore, that until the eve of the foundation of the French Republic, Marat though violently opposed to Louis XVI personally as king, favored the institution of monarchy as the form of government most desirable for France.   Marat on August 10, 1792 was, then, an enemy of Louis XVI, of the Constitution of 1791, and of the newly established government.   But he was not yet a republican.   Vacillating, however, between hatred of the monarch and distrust of the republic, he had been led to suggest certain measures to prevent the failure of the Revolution that committed him neither to monarchism nor republicanism.   And these measures we must now consider.

CHAPTER IV

THE term *French Revolution* has had a varied interpretation. To contemporary as well as to later writers it has signified entirely different things, both in what it set out to do and in what it ought to have done. For Mounier and Robespierre, De Tocqueville and Jaurès, it had two, perhaps four, greatly divergent meanings. Marat used the word *revolution* frequently, but it is difficult to determine whether he ever stopped to consider exactly what he meant by it. Since the beginning of the Revolution, when he had stated in definite terms in his *Offrande à la patrie* and his *Plan de Constitution* what he wanted the Revolution to accomplish, he had not given much space to constructive criticism. Most of his words had been penned against other people and their schemes. But he was not entirely without a plan for the reconstruction of France, and what it was can be gleaned from statements made at various times during the careers of the National and Legislative Assemblies. By the time we are now considering, the word *revolution* had begun to represent for Marat a very definite ideal.

The feeling of sympathy for the indigent classes that had moved Marat in the years before the Revolution remained with him until his assassination at the hands of Charlotte Corday. There is a touch of pathos in the fact that, in order to gain admittance to his presence, his assassin had planned to take advantage of his well-known pity for the down-trodden with the plea, "It is sufficient that I am unhappy to have a right to your protection." As far as Marat had been able, he had sincerely tried, often in an awkward, blundering manner, to be the Friend of the People that he boldly advertised he was. He repeatedly maintained that he had earned the title of *Ami du Peuple*, and he was known by it even in official circles. It was the people, he claimed, to whom he had devoted his life and fortune, in whose behalf he had made all his enemies and endured racking persecution, for whose sake during more than three years he had taken no more than a quarter of an hour's recreation, for whom he was willing to die. It was a sacred duty for him to plead the cause

> of the needy, of those workers who form the sanest, the most useful part of the people, without whom society could not exist a single day; of these precious citizens upon whom weigh all the burdens of the state and who enjoy none of its advantages; of those unfortunates who look with disdain upon the scoundrel who grows fat by their sweat and who rudely rebuff the publicans who drink their blood in cups of gold; of those unfortunates who in the midst of the luxury, pomp, and pleasure which the lord who oppresses them enjoys in their presence, have as their share only labor, misery, grief, and hunger.

On behalf of these miserable wretches he demanded change. Fifty years before Louis Blanc was heard of, he advocated that the confiscated property of the church be made into public workshops for the employment of the poor, and invented other schemes for enterprises at government expense to insure employment to the workers. At one time he argued for a more equal distribution of all land. He looked for the eventual establishment of complete equality of wealth, but until that happy day he thought there ought to be a public fund, managed by some upright citizen, from which the heads of families who were insolvent through no fault of their own might be enabled to pay their debts. On another occasion, when the National Assembly was discussing Necker's suggestion of a direct tax of twenty-five per cent on all property, he pointed out the obvious unfairness of such a levy on the poor and brought forward a detailed scheme for a progressive income tax. The motto of his *Journal de la République française*, which we shall find taking the place of the *Ami du Peuple*, boldly declared in dactyllic hexameter that he wanted the wealth of the rich reduced for the benefit of the poor—*Ut redeat miseris, abeat fortuna superbis.* On May 4, 1793, when he was a member of the Convention, his efforts resulted in the passing of a decree to aid the families of volunteers at the front out of public funds. Four days before his death he still bemoaned the fact that the confiscated lands of the nobility and clergy had been squandered without any attempt having been made to alleviate the sufferings of the poor.

During all this period he also called for an elaborate program of what we should now call labor legislation. He advocated the abolition of the antiquated *jurandes*, an apprenticeship of six or seven years, and a wage sufficient to enable a workingman, after three years of faithful service, to go into business for himself. If such a program now would seem extravagant, it must be remembered that in the eighteenth century France was almost entirely under the domestic system of industry, manufacture being carried on by small groups in small shops with comparatively inexpensive tools, and a small sum was enough to set up an independent establishment. On the other hand, certain measures which were harmful in one way or another to the interests of the lower classes met with Marat's disapproval. The proposals requiring universal military service for four years, the agitation for the continuance of imprisonment for debt, the mammoth allowances granted to the King and his subordinates, the creation of *assignats* only in high denominations, the delay in the abolition of tariff duties between points inside France—all these (as we have already seen in the case of some of them) he assailed, because they seemed to him to be projects that fell very heavily upon the workers while they affected the rich favorably if at all. As decrees of this nature became more frequent and those that he proposed received no serious attention, he began to believe that only through their own endeavors would the people obtain what they sought. In December 1790 he laid down as "a general rule":

> If you want to have a popular undertaking succeed, address yourself to workingmen, to simple laborers. They are the only ones who have courage and feeling.

The question might well be asked: Was Marat a socialist? Had he lived at a time when socialism was a well defined political program and not at a time when even the word *socialism* was unknown, it is reasonably safe to assume that he would have been one of its foremost exponents. Under the circumstances in which he found himself, however, his socialism was but a vague, uncrystallized longing for social justice; he did nothing more than to advocate a liberal policy of social legislation and, like his mentor Rousseau, was merely a harbinger of socialism. The fear of communism (*la loi agraire*) was, without good cause, quite prevalent during the French Revolution. Marat, whose loose use of startling language laid him open to all manner of charges, was sometimes accused of preaching the agrarian law. But, as we have seen, until August 1792, he was a monarchist. At no time did he conceive of a state run by a working class for the exclusive benefit of the working class or by the peasants for the peasants. He himself, in a *Profession of Faith* issued on March 30, 1793, in reply to the numerous accusations of his enemies, repudiated the charge of ever having championed an agrarian law, describing it as "destructive of all civil society." This apparently indicates that on the rare occasions when he did preach an unmistakably socialistic doctrine, he was not prepared to carry it to a radical conclusion.

Nevertheless, Jaurès, perhaps the most famous of the socialist historians of the French Revolution, has stated that one cannot study the history of the worker's movement without understanding the significance of Marat in that movement. It was very largely through him that the proletariat of Paris attained some degree of class consciousness. For whatever influence he had was always upon the common people. It was the radical district of the Cordeliers that first offered him its protection on the occasion of the *affaire de Marat* of January 22, 1790, and supported him throughout the remainder of his career. Another stronghold of his influence was the Club of the Jacobins, by whom he was continually lionized, meeting only once with severe censure, and whose president he was for a short period (April 5–21, 1793). His staunchest personal followers were the large number of correspondents—workers and common-folk—who flooded his paper with letters. His greatest admirers among his fellow-journalists were likewise editors who championed the cause of the lower classes—Camille Desmoulins of the *Révolutions de France et de Brabant*, who considered him, "without doubt the one of all the journalists who has best served the Revolution"; Prudhomme of the *Révolution de Paris*, who feigned contempt of him but nevertheless borrowed his ideas and words verbatim without acknowledging their source; and Fréron of the *Orateur du Peuple* who frankly imitated his manner, speech, and opinions and allowed him to edit the *Orateur du Peuple* on several occasions. Friend and foe alike agreed that the proletariat rallied around him.

It must not be thought, however, that the support Marat received from these various quarters was constant and unflinching. In fact, as has already been pointed out, from January 1790 to August 1792, he was frequently forced to flee or to hide from his enemies, and, as a candidate for the Legislative Assembly in September 1791, he had been able to command only two votes.   But after the Revolution passed into the hands of the lower classes of Paris in August 1792, Marat's influence kept constantly on the ascendant; and in general it is true that in the period following the founding of the *Ami du Peuple* both his sympathy for the lower classes and their confidence in him were steadily increasing.   In view of all this, it is easy to glean what Marat thought the Revolution ought to achieve.   It was to mean a change from an unenlightened despotism to a government that should devote a large part of its endeavors to ameliorating the condition of the common people, the workers, and the poor.   He now desired a social, as well as a political reform, one which should rise up from below and not seep down from above.   This was an attitude quite different from that which he had held at the outbreak of the Revolution, but because of the constant danger of reaction, the omnipresent fear of counter-revolution, his sentiments had undergone an important change.

But how was this new conception of the Revolution to be realized?   One would be led to venture that his answer would have been: "Through the people!"   And so to a certain extent it was.   But Marat, Friend of the People, had little faith in the people's intelligence or ability.   His conviction was that the Revolution was to be accomplished by them only if necessary, only if all the other expedients failed. Even now, although he thought he saw King, nobility, clergy, and bourgeoisie alike exerting every effort to effect a counter-revolution, his mind was not definitely made up.   He debated with himself:

> Expect nothing from rich and opulent men, from men brought up in luxury and pleasures, from greedy men who love only gold.   It is not of old slaves that free citizens are made.   There remain only the farmers, small merchants, artisans, and workers, laborers

and proletariat, as the insolent rich call them, to form a free people, impatient of the yoke of oppression and always ready to break
it. But these people are not educated; and nothing is so difficult
as to educate them. It is even an impossible task to-day when a
thousand venal pens are working only to mislead them in order to
put them again in chains.

No! The French were not capable of achieving liberty by
themselves. What change had been brought about in their
status had been accomplished by a series of fortunate accidents, by a "tutelary god" who watched over the safety
of the friends of liberty. They themselves were "senseless";
"vile slaves"; "blind, credulous, confident, simple, patient";
"so vain, so foolish, so imbecile, that it is almost impossible
to save them." They lacked the love of equality, a virtue
so essential for democracy; they were incapable of concerted
action; their vanity and frivolity rendered them unfit for
freedom. A republic for such people was entirely out of the
question.

Moreover, Marat, nourished as he was on eighteenth century philosophical traditions, seemed unable to conceive of
France as a republic: it was too large and its government too
complex. The republics that had existed until that time—
Athens, Rome, the Italian and German cities, the Swiss Can-
tons, Holland, and the United States of America—had been
either city-states or federated governments. Countries of
the extent of France had always been monarchies. Therefore, whenever Marat spoke of a republican form of government in France, it was with a mental picture of France
broken up into small federated states. Such a conception was
hateful to him, so hateful that once, when he wished to
stamp an act of the National Assembly as unspeakably ridiculous, he had said that it was as preposterous as for the
provinces of France to transform themselves into small and

federated republics. Should such a thing have occurred, he would have expected nothing from it but a renewal of the old feudal strife that had once torn France asunder.

But if France could not become a republic, if the people were unable to work out their own salvation, if the monarchy was too selfish and corrupt to aid them to do so, some solution must be found. And so Marat was obliged to devise revolutionary measures long before most contemporary thinkers had found them necessary. At first he had insisted upon the permanence of the Paris District Assemblies. These, as bodies of citizens originally called together to elect the representatives of Paris to the Estates General but still keeping their organization after their tasks were performed, could avoid the pitfalls that would endanger individuals and could keep more effective watch upon the National Assembly. After the suppression of the Districts and the erection of the Paris Sections, he thought the same results could be obtained by patriotic clubs, to be open to tried and acknowledged patriots. Their task would be to unite the efforts of the people, to direct the movements of their respective quarters, and to take decisive action in suppressing public enemies and in all other matters pertaining to the general welfare. The chief among these clubs was to be the Society of the Avengers of the Law, whose proposed name renders obvious its proposed functions. Of this club, Marat wanted Robespierre, Dubois de Crancé, and Reubel to be the founders. By thus advocating the general formation of patriotic organizations (June 1790-March 1791) before any of them had begun to assume the important rôles that they later played (the Jacobins and the Cordeliers still were isolated cases and at their inception were more bourgeois than popular), Marat earned for himself the title of "father of the fraternal societies," bestowed by his contemporary Fréron and endorsed by a recent historian of the club movement.[1]   While he was still suggesting this policy, he kept urging another of perhaps greater value.   Along with the other institutions of the Ancient Regime the old law courts were now considered inadequate.   Marat's own unpleasant experience with the Châtelet was enough to convince him of that, even if further proof were lacking.   A new tribunal for the trial of political offenders must be formed.   He had counselled such a step as early as the second number of the *Ami du Peuple* and never yielded the point until, in March 1793, the Revolutionary Tribunal was established.   In the meantime he kept up a spasmodic propaganda for a reorganization of the judicial hierarchy.   His *Lettre . . . contenant quelques réflexions sur l'ordre judiciare*, written in April 1790, while he was spending his first enforced absence from France in England, not only contained an attack on his inveterate foe, the Châtelet, but also presented his views regarding a new tribunal that he proposed.   The Assembly, he argued, here and elsewhere, had a power to create a court composed of a few of France's most distinguished and upright citizens, to be named by public vote, before whom any citizen might hail any other regardless of their relative social positions; the judges, who must always be honest and capable men, were to be elected by popular vote; its special task would be to punish public officials who had abused their authority or office; it was in every conceivable way to be rendered independent of the king.   Marat expected wonderful achievements from such a judicial body, perhaps even the complete disappearance of the enemies of the Revolution.   As he had anticipated, however, when the National Assembly did take up the matter of judicial reform, its decree was wholly unacceptable.   He complained (October 30, 1790) that the ultimate choice

---

[1] Mathiez, *Le Club des Cordeliers,* p. 18; see also article by same in *Annales révolutionnaires,* I, pp. 660–664.

of the judges of the High Court was left to the king; that the legislature was to name the places of their sessions; that only those whose taxes amounted to a *marc d'argent* were eligible for office in the new judiciary. For a moment he looked to the Legislative Assembly to erect a better tribunal, but that Assembly did nothing; and he was to receive no satisfaction until the Convention in March 1793 established the Revolutionary Tribunal, which he soon pronounced "one of the great means of saving the country."

In the meantime, after his disappointment on finding that the National Assembly had created what he considered an inadequate system of courts, Marat had adopted a new policy. The clubs were ineffective; the authorities had emasculated his plan for a revolutionary tribunal; and meanwhile, he felt, the people, leaderless and groping, were further from an amelioration of their pitiable state than ever. They must be given a leader. He had seen them conquer, he said, on July 14 and on October 5–6 and then allow their temporary advantages to slip through their fingers because they had no capable guidance. Often, in blood-curdling tones, he had himself summoned them to revolt, to burn the Senate house, to purge it of its suspect members, to mutilate and destroy individual traitors. In November 1790, after the Nancy and Belfort affairs, his cries for such popular measures occurred almost daily, so passionate and angry as almost to justify the charge, frequently made, that he was a homicidal maniac. But he had been forced to realize how helpless and blind the multitude was without a leader and that consequently no popular uprising would be successful unless skilfully prepared and conducted. So he resorted to a policy which was to be his greatest contribution to the revolutionary thought of his epoch, although it was neither original nor practicable: the people must choose for themselves a dictator to pilot them safely through the storm of the Revolution.

Here again, though it cannot be proved conclusively, there is good reason to assume that Marat borrowed his idea from Rousseau. In the *Social Contract*, Rousseau sets forth this theory of dictatorship:

The inflexibility of laws, which prevents them from conforming to events, can, in certain cases, make them dangerous and cause the ruin of the state in a crisis. Order and the slow movement of formalities demand a lapse of time which circumstances sometimes do not allow. It is possible for a thousand mischances to occur which the legislator has not foreseen. . . . It is not necessary therefore to desire to strengthen political institutions to the extent of making it impossible to suspend their power. But it is only the greatest dangers that can counter-balance that of tampering with public order, and the sacred power of the laws ought never to be checked except when the welfare of the country is at stake. In such rare and obvious cases, public safety is provided for by a special act which entrusts the care of it to the most worthy individual. This commission can be given in two ways, according to the nature of the danger. If to remedy it, it is sufficient to increase the activity of the government, it is concentrated in the hands of one or two of its members. Thus it is not the authority of the laws that is changed but only the form of the administration of them. But if the danger is such that the machinery of the laws is an obstacle to be protected from, then a supreme chief is named who silences all the laws and suspends for a moment the sovereign authority. In such cases the general will is not in doubt; it is evident that the chief intention of the people is that the state should not perish. In this way the suspension of the legislative authority does not abolish it. The magistrate who silences it can not make it speak; he dominates it without being able to replace it; he can do everything except make laws.

Such was Rousseau's doctrine, and so similar was Marat's to become that, even without knowing the influence of Rousseau upon Marat, it would be logical to surmise that the theory of the one was derived from that of the other. But what Rousseau had said merely as an *obiter dictum*, Marat adopted and made his entire political creed and dogma.

When Marat first began to advocate a dictatorship, he wished it to be employed only when treason reached the point where the revolutionary tribunal which he had suggested could no longer cope with it.   The earliest mention of the possible need of a dictator is to be found in his caustic address of October 5, 1789, which helped to bring about the March to Versailles.   But it was not until the appearance of the *Appel à la nation*, written during his stay in England in 1790, that he first called upon the French "to name for a short time a supreme dictator, to put him at the head of the public forces, and to intrust to him the punishment of the guilty."   Here he apparently thought that the dictator might work in conjunction with his *tribunal d'état*.   But by the end of July 1790, he had begun to understand that a supreme dictator could be substituted altogether for other revolutionary measures but could not merely supplement them.

Having once conceived of the necessity for a dictator, Marat continued to agitate for one until the establishment of the French Republic made it necessary for him to adopt a new course.   Before June 21, 1791, the day on which the King took flight from Paris, he had frequently called for a dictator, but his demands had not been definite or insistent. The escape of the King, however, rendered immediate action imperative and drew from Marat a clear-cut statement of his policy in a stern appeal to the people:

> Only one way remains for you to drag yourselves from the brink to which your unworthy chiefs have brought you. That is to name a military tribune, a supreme dictator, to lay hands upon the principal known traitors. . . . Let your choice fall upon the citizen who has shown to this day the most enlightenment, zeal, and loyalty. Swear inviolable devotion to him and obey him religiously in all that he will command in order to get rid of your mortal enemies. . . . A tribune, a military tribune, or you are lost beyond recovery. Until now I have done all that lay within human power to save you. If you neglect this salutary advice,

which is all that is left for me to give you, I have nothing more
to say to you and I take leave of you forever.

On the next day he repeated this exhortation with similar
threats. But in vain! The people of France, with only a
low rumble of protest from radical quarters, accepted their
ruler again. But Marat, despite his menaces, did not abandon them. Throughout the remainder of the year, as his
fear of counter-revolution grew, he continued to call for
popular movements under a dictator. When Bouillé announced that he would march upon Paris to protect the King,
when the Massacre of the Champ de Mars shocked the universal sense of justice, when further attempts of Louis to
flee and new schemes of conspiracy were rumored, Marat
called for a military tribune or a supreme dictator. It has
already been noted that he spent the early part of 1792 in
England, where he had gone to take refuge after the Legislative Assembly had added to the disgust that he had felt
for the Constituent Assembly. As we have seen, after his
return, there followed a short period of enforced silence.
But he renewed his propaganda for the tribunate with the
resumption of the *Ami du Peuple* in April 1792. His apprehension that the war between France and her continental
neighbors, which was imminent at the time of his return,
was part of a plot to restore the Ancient Regime led him
to insist again upon a dictator who would take strong measures
to prevent the outbreak of hostilities. On July 8, 1792, he
published a clear and decisive statement that may be regarded as a summary of his entire dictatorship program.
Only by popular insurrection, he asserted, could the ills of
the country be rectified, but the people needed "a clear-
sighted, firm, honest, and incorruptible chief" to guide their
actions. Ten days later he urged the Departments as well
as Paris to support this policy. It is clear, therefore, that

by this time, the Revolution had ceased to be for Marat merely a series of reforms already effected or to be effected by the King and the various assemblies; it was now a movement for the welfare of the lower classes, to be participated in by all of the lower classes throughout France, under the leadership of a dictator chosen by themselves and implicitly trusted by them.

In the ensuing months (July-August 1792) the republican party in France gained strength day by day. But Marat still clung to the dictatorship, seemingly oblivious to the significant change that was being wrought in the political sentiments of the people around him. The *Ami du Peuple* which, after his going into hiding from the police authorities because of the decree of accusation passed against him on May 3, 1792, had appeared only twenty-nine times between that date and August 10, contained no allusion to the prevalent idea of popular government; the very word *république* did not occur. The new duties that we shall find devolving upon him during the month of September as a member of the city's government kept him so busy that there are but few issues from his press before September 22, 1792. What little we have contains nothing to indicate that he desired or even suspected the declaration of a republic. In fact, in a statement written on September 20, the very day the National Convention, to which Marat himself had been elected a deputy, began its sessions, he repeated his demand for a dictator:

> In view of the temper of the majority of the deputies of the National Convention, I despair of the public welfare. If within the first eight sessions all of the foundations of the constitution have not been laid, expect nothing more of your representatives. You are ruined forever. Fifty years of anarchy await you and you will come out of it only through a dictator, a true patriot and statesman. Oh, chattering people, if you knew how to act!

On the next day, when the issue of the *Ami du Peuple* containing this comment was put on sale, the Convention abolished monarchy. Whatever else Marat was, then, he certainly was not one of the founders of the Republic.

The dictatorship that Marat advocated was not of the Cæsarian or Napoleonic type. One of his reasons for opposing the declaration of war against the Empire and Prussia had been that it would result in just such a dictatorship. Following the teachings of Rousseau, he wanted a tribunate limited both in the time of its duration and its powers. He spoke of it as "momentary"—at one time lasting "for a day," at another "for three days only," at another "for six weeks," and so on, not necessarily progressively. The dictator was to guide the people in bringing their enemies to justice, to aid them in drawing the Revolution to a successful conclusion. At first Marat spoke of granting him power "without limitations" (August 30, 1791), but later (April 19, 1792) decided that he ought to have unlimited power to crush the chief conspirators but no power to dominate the country. When his work was done, he was to relinquish his office and become lost in the common throng. The strange thing is that while Marat was thus advocating government by a dictator, he said nothing to indicate that he was not still a monarchist at heart. He evidently desired a return to the monarchical form of government after the dictator had succeeded in laying the foundations of an enlightened government.

Marat has been accused of wishing to make several different men dictator. We may dismiss the accusation that it was the Duke of Brunswick, who for a time was seriously considered in certain quarters as a candidate for the French throne, with its denial by Marat; it has no support other than the charge made by his enemies, the Rolands. Much the same may be said of the contention that it was the Duke

of Orleans. At the time that Marat was urging the dictatorship, as well as after he had abandoned his open support
of it, he attacked Orleans as "a prince of the blood" and a
member "of the court party." Furthermore, after the flight
of the King in June 1791, when Marat suggested a regency
to take the place of Louis XVI until the Dauphin should
come of age, he specified particularly that the regent must
not be of the Capetian house, mentioning the Duke of Orleans by name. The request that Marat made of the Duke
for money to publish certain books was public and can not
be considered as a demand for remuneration for conspiracy,[1]
especially since there is no proof that Marat ever received the
money; certainly the books that he hoped to publish if he got
it never were published.

Nor was it Robespierre whom Marat designated for the
dictatorship, as several of the enemies of both have charged.
True, Marat had been an ardent admirer of Robespierre from
the very beginning of the Revolution. He often called him
the only honest and incorruptible deputy in the National Assembly and once suggested him as the only fit tutor of the
Dauphin. But Robespierre himself denied that he had ever
conspired with Marat for the dictatorship and Marat corroborated him a number of times, claiming on one occasion to
have met Robespierre only once and to have been convinced
then by Robespierre's protest against his own fiery language
that while Robespierre was a good patriot and deputy, he
"lacked both the views and the audacity of a stateman."
Robespierre gave the same account of this interview, though
he did not come to the same conclusion regarding his own
ability as a statesman.

There is but little more likelihood that it was Danton

---

[1] *Marat à Louis Philippe Joseph d'Orléans, Prince français,* in Chevremont,
Placards de Marat, erroneously dated by Chevremont September 2, 1792, but
really of September 10 (see Charavay, *Assemblées électorales de Paris,* III, p
606, fn.).

whom Marat had chosen to honor with the title of tribune and dictator. Marat owed to Danton a debt of gratitude for his part in the Marat Affair; and in those early days Marat described Danton only in superlatives. Indeed throughout the remainder of the life of Marat, Danton was one of the very few to receive favor in Marat's eyes, even rivalling Robespierre in this respect. Once upon learning of Marie Antoinette's treasonable activities, he urged that Danton, who was already Minister of Justice, be made Minister of the Interior and President of the Executive Council with a deciding vote and influence in case of deadlock. This suggestion, coming as it did in the midst of Marat's agitation for a dictator, might be interpreted as a bid in Danton's behalf. But here again denials were made by both men. Marat admitted that while he thought that Danton had the necessary qualifications for a dictator, Danton himself preferred a *chaise percée* to a dictatorial throne. The charges against Marat would have been much more effective if they had insisted upon Marat's conspiracy with one man rather than with several at one time.[1] If it had been Marat's intention to place any one of these men on a dictatorial throne, he probably would have perceived that to assure the success of his campaign it would have been better to focus all attention on one candidate than to dissipate it among several.

Yet he must have had someone in mind, perhaps without himself being aware of it, when he inaugurated his campaign for a dictator. Whom? The most likely explanation is that Marat planned to have the dictatorship for himself. On July 26, 1790, he enumerated the things he would do if he were tribune. In November he expressed the wish that the people might have "a tribune who had the soul of their

---

[1] Even Aulard fails to see this. In his *French Revolution* he says in one place that Marat dreamed "perhaps" of himself as dictator; in another "probably" of Danton; in a third "possibly" of the Duc d'Orleans.

Friend." In the following December he published a letter from one of his readers urging him to continue his course; "and some day the country will put you at the head of its true defenders." In view of the fact that Marat admitted that he edited the letters which he printed in his journal, it is significant that the letter containing these words was allowed to appear in the *Ami du Peuple*. On at least four subsequent occasions, he again described in detail what he could accomplish if he were tribune. On September 2, 1791, expressing his confidence in the line troops, he said:

> They need only a chief, a man of head and heart. If the purest sense of civic duty counts for anything at all, I would want a friend of the people [*un ami du peuple*] for them. I would give one of my fingers right now that they might know my sentiments and put them to the test.

This statement is ambiguous, but the ambiguity seems deliberate and studied. Taken alone it might mean nothing at all. Together with the opinions already cited, it seems to be but another insinuation in the direction Marat wanted to go. But two months before this (July 8, 1791), in a statement already referred to as admirably summing up his whole attitude on the dictatorship, he gave the clearest evidence that it was himself he advocated as dictator:

> What means are left us to-day to put an end to the evils that overwhelm us? I repeat, there is no other than popular execution and we shall have to have recourse to that even after fifty years of anarchy, dissension, and disaster, if we should ever again resist the despots sworn against us and if we should ever wish to be free at last. Only two objections of little weight have been offered in opposition to this plan. One is that it would be impossible to find a single citizen who would fill any office if he had perpetually to fear popular executions. I answer that there is an infallible means of avoiding them. That is to show oneself a good patriot. . . . The other is that it would be dangerous to abandon to themselves a blind multitude. But what prevents giv-

ing them a staunch, upright, and incorruptible chief? Where
find him? Must you be told? You know a man who aspires
only to the glory of sacrificing himself for the welfare of our
country. You have seen him at work a long time. But I had
better be on guard against allowing his disinterestedness to be suspected, in case he should ever become the object of your choice and
has not himself lost all hope of any longer serving your cause.

A single one of these statements would be sufficient to create
suspicion regarding Marat's lack of self-interest in advocating his policy; all of them together make that suspicion a certainty.

It must be admitted that Marat emphatically denied the
presence of any personal ambition in his support of the dictatorship. These denials were not made, however, until after
he had been accused of selfish motives by his enemies and had
become the target of frequent attacks on that score. Furthermore, in several of these denials, Marat confused ambitious
purposes with selfish purposes and argued, not so much that he
had not wanted the dictatorship for himself, as that his end
in preaching that policy was to aid the people rather than to
aggrandize himself. In one of these disclaimers (November
8, 1792), he asserted that it would have been fatuous for him
to aspire to a dictatorship, since he realized how hopelessly
without friends and supporters he was. But in the same
breath he declared that if he had only wished it, he might
have been made tribune of the people on the day of the flight
of the King; what caused him to hesitate was that he bore in
mind the fickleness of the mob, which lifts a man to the clouds
on one day only to make sport of him the next. These two
statements contradict each other and, furthermore, neither of
them is true. For while Marat was not so entirely devoid
of followers that he could not on several occasions have made
an effective bid for the dictatorship, the day of the flight of
the King certainly was not one of these. The fact, already

noted, that Marat's two threats to abandon the people of France unless they chose a military tribune went entirely unheeded shows that they were not prepared for such a revolutionary measure at that time.   Indeed, a consideration of Marat's statements on June 22–23, 1791, immediately after the flight of the King, and this one of November 8, 1792 makes possible an interesting speculation.   On June 22, 1791, he vigorously insisted that the people name a military tribune and on June 23 repeated the exhortation; but the people disregarded his prayers.   Nevertheless, on November 8, 1792, he alleged that, had he wished, he might have become dictator of France on the day of the flight of the King (June 21, 1791). Is it possible that Marat, looking back, over a year later, on the events of June 21–23, 1791, read into them as a fact something that was then merely a desire?   Was the wish father to the thought?   "Let your choice fall upon the citizen who has shown to this day the most enlightened zeal and loyalty," he had then said.   And it will be remembered that Robert said of him that he suffered from the malady of "believing that he was the only patriot of France."

In still another denial that he had wanted the dictatorship for himself, Marat reiterated his protest that he would not have taken the office had it been tendered to him, because he could not have been sure that the people would have continued to support him.   But he forgot that this popular capriciousness was an obstacle that would have had to be encountered regardless of whether he himself or someone else—for he must have had somebody in mind—held the post of dictator.   Besides, Marat would not have been true to himself had he declined the dictatorship if it had been offered to him.   For the Friend of the People was ambitious; he asked nothing better than to become the "Boss" of the People as well.   He had no doubt that he was the best man for the position, and his frequent counsel to the people indicated how extremely willing he was to act the part.   The time was shortly to come when Marat would be the dictator of the people *de facto*, if not *de nomine*, and when he would use his power to the utmost.   For the present, until September 22, 1792, the day on which the first French Republic was established, he kept dinning the cry for a tribune into the ears of any who cared to listen, all but daring to come out frankly with the demand for his own nomination.

September 1792 was filled with new activities for Marat. On September 2, he was invited to become a member of the *Comité de Surveillance* of the Commune.   That same day saw the beginning of the terrible September Massacres, for the instigation of which Marat has frequently been held responsible.   While the dire threats of the manifesto of the Duke of Brunswick were still fresh in the minds of Frenchmen a series of unfortunate accidents brought their enemies almost to the gates of Paris.   Lafayette deserted.   Lille, after a gallant resistance, surrendered to the Prussians. Longwy fell on August 2; and on the morning of the day that the Massacres commenced, Verdun was captured.   In Paris a feeling of panic seized many hearts.   For no well-founded reason, rumors of a plot on the part of the prisoners in the Paris jails to break out and take a bloody vengeance on their persecutors had gained wide-spread credence.   The volunteers of Paris, fearing that in their absence at the front the royalists would actually succeed in gaining their freedom and would fall upon their defenseless families, began the work of slaughtering prisoners.   Among those who were impelled by fear for their families' safety and by hatred of royalism there were doubtless a number of ruffians who desired nothing more than bloodshed and sadistic satisfaction.   The events of those days have ever since been branded with the name of the September Massacres.   The number of "executions" has been estimated at figures varying from nine hundred to sixteen hundred. Comparatively speaking, only a few took part in the actual butchery, but almost the whole city was aware of what was going on and did nothing to prevent it. To what an extent was Marat more guilty than others?

Marat had, of course, time and again urged popular executions. Over and over he had called for preposterously large numbers of heads, varying from five hundred to one hundred thousand actually demanded under existing circumstances and five hundred thousand suggested as possibly necessary at some future time if matters continued to grow worse. On May 27, 1791, for example, he announced that

> eleven months ago five hundred heads would have sufficed; to-day fifty thousand would be necessary; perhaps five hundred thousand will fall before the end of the year. France will have been flooded with blood, but it will not be more free because of it.

He generally dealt in round numbers. But there is absolutely no proof that he ever asked for such an unusual number as two hundred and sixty thousand heads, which Barbaroux, his disciple in the days of his scientific achievements but later one of his bitterest enemies, insisted that he required, or any of the other ridiculous numbers, sometimes quoted as high as eight hundred thousand, that he has been charged with having demanded; Michelet, for example, wrote that Marat in his last days insisted upon the ridiculous figure of 273,000 heads. It is doubtful whether Marat ever stopped to realize the significance of the numbers he used. Figures seemed never to have had much meaning for him. When he wished to be emphatic he used an exorbitantly high number; when he wished to be derogatory he used a correspondingly low one. He would demand a certain number of heads at one time, a lower one the next, a higher one the next, and so on, the figures varying from day to day with no continuous progression. While he kept remonstrating that the situation was steadily becoming worse and clamored for heads, the number he wanted fluctuated up and down with each successive cry. Marat himself always claimed that his motive in demanding so large a number of executions was to arrest the counter-revolution once and for all and to prevent the proscription by the Bourbonists, in case of their success, of a greater number than he had ever dared suggest. Thus, to him, what others called his thirst for blood was really clemency.

Moreover, there is good reason to believe that Marat used exaggeration deliberately, in order to create a stronger impression upon his readers. He denied this himself; in a conversation with Robespierre, which he reported in his issue of May 3, 1792, he insisted that he meant every word he said. Even here, however, he seemed to realize that a large part of his popularity depended upon his audacious and fiery language. He could not, of course, be expected to admit openly that he employed his peculiar style of expression only for effect in the paper that was published for the very audience that he wanted to impress. But those who knew him held a different opinion. Half a year later, Basire announced to the Jacobin Club that Marat had confidentially acknowledged to him:

> I ask overmuch of the people because I know that the people are looking for a bargain; but my hand would wither at my side rather than write, if I were sure that the people would carry out what I tell them to do.

That Marat exaggerated intentionally in order to lend emphasis to his words was also the opinion of his fellow-journalist Prudhomme. His view is by no means complimentary to Marat, but it at least exonerates him from actually meaning to bring about bloodshed:

> Marat, despite his lists of proscriptions, loves blood no more than anyone else. Dominated by an excessive self-love, he does not

want to say what others have said and in the manner they have said it. If anyone has discovered a truth, a principle, before him, in order not to fall behind he passes beyond and falls into exaggeration. Often he borders upon folly, upon atrocity, but he professes principles that the ill-intentioned fear and abhor.

Panis, a colleague of Marat on the Committee of Surveillance, expressed a slightly different feeling, which, nevertheless, also serves as testimony that Marat did not mean all of his cries for execution to be taken literally:

With his ardent spirit and lively imagination, always bent upon the same object, is it astonishing that he says extraordinary things? But he would be the first to protect with his own body the most criminal of the aristocrats. He has provoked the most terrible vengeances, but it was to frighten rascals, in order that a salutary fear might turn them from their frightful projects.

Barras also offers an amusing bit of evidence to support Panis' statement that Marat would have protected even aristocrats. He claims to have seen a mob manhandling an imprudent wretch, dressed in the despised costume of the Ancient Regime, whom they were preparing to slaughter, when Marat happened along. Taking in the situation at a glance, the Friend of the People removed the fellow from the hands of his tormentors, gave him a hearty kick, and while everybody laughed, allowed him to run away. In a very similar way, Marat is reported also to have saved Théroigne de Méricourt when that stalwart feminist was attacked by a mob of angry women. The somewhat too optimistic Fabre d'Eglantine says of Marat's "little escapes" of fatuity "that he was always the first to repress them and to regain his natural good nature."

In view of such testimony there is some reason to doubt that Marat was entirely in earnest in all of his exhortations to violence. It was probably his intention thus "to ask overmuch of the people" on August 19, 1792, when he cried to them to "rise and let the blood of traitors flow again.   It is the only means of saving the Fatherland." Put to the sword all the prisoners at the Abbaye, especially the Swiss officers and their accomplices of August 10. What need of a trial? Had they not been taken in arms against the country on August 10? Whether Marat meant to be taken at his word or not, the appeal fell upon eager ears, for the people of Paris were already in a frenzy. He must have sensed the situation, and if he did not want to have his words taken at their face value, he was indiscreet to have spoken. But even so, this plea for action was made two weeks before the massacres began and in that interval there was no similar demand in his paper.

Nevertheless, Mortimer-Ternaux, one of the foremost authorities on the history of the Reign of Terror, maintains that the September Massacres were premeditated, and chiefly by Marat. In addition to several quotations from memoirs unfavorable to Marat, the only evidence of a serious nature that he brings forward to prove this point is a document, signed only by Panis and Sargent of the Committee of Police and Surveillance, urging the trial of all prisoners at the Abbaye, with the exception of one Abbé Lenfant. Since this document is dated September 2, it is possible that it was issued after the Massacres were already well under way and with the single purpose of saving this particular Abbé, who was the brother of one of the members of the Committee of Surveillance. If we agree, as some authorities do, however, that this appeal was the immediate cause of the horrifying events of September 2–5, Marat can not be regarded as directly responsible for it. Since he was made, together with six others, a member of the Committee only on that very day, his signature is not to be found affixed to it. There is room for speculation as to whether Marat was not unofficially connected with the Committee before his actual appointment and therefore whether he was not the instigator of the disastrous appeal. But though such a connection may have existed (Marat had been named the official reporter of the Commune's activities but never did anything in that capacity), no conclusive evidence can be adduced to prove it. Consequently the most that can be fairly said is that, if Marat was responsible for the September Massacres at all, it was only indirectly, through the influence of his well-aired opinions in general and of his call to arms of August 19 in particular. His own account of the Massacres states that, when they began, he was surprised and unprepared for them and that with the other members of the Committee of Police and Surveillance he put forth every effort to save the petty delinquents in the prisons.

One person whom he evidently wished to have punished for his part in the work of the National Assembly was Adrien Duport. Danton interfered in Duport's behalf, however, and after a fierce altercation, Marat yielded. Otherwise the friendly but never fervid relations between these two might have come entirely to a close upon that occasion. This Duport incident has been made much of by writers unfavorably disposed toward Marat to show his pernicious activity in the Committee of Surveillance. That it was an unsavory episode none but the blindest apologist for Marat would deny. But after all, it was the business of the Committee of Police and Surveillance to bring suspects to trial; and Duport, who had shared with Barnave and the Lameths the confidence of Marie Antoinette, was not above Marat's jealous suspicion. Nor is there any good reason to believe that Marat was any more assiduous in obtaining arrests than his colleagues. The issuance of a warrant for the apprehension of Roland and Brissot can not be proven to have been exclusively Marat's work, as has sometimes been charged. Even Danton, who countermanded it, put the blame for it upon "that

mad Committee" and threatened to "bring *them* to reason!"
He was not feeling kindly toward Marat at this moment, and
would certainly have named him, especially if he had thought
it justified. Nobody at that time spoke of the Massacres
as having originated with Marat alone. Afterwards Pétion
and Maton de la Varenne, both rank outsiders and enemies
of Marat, maintained in their memoirs that Marat was the
guiding evil genius of the Committee. Their testimony,
however, is counterbalanced by that of Panis, head of the
Committee, who declared that "in the midst of the Committee
of Surveillance Marat did not have a special influence; his
advice never prevailed over that of any other patriot."

To have played the leading part in any popular movement
would have been a feather in Marat's cap. That he was not
ashamed of whatever connection he had with this one can be
deduced from his signature to the circular letter of September
3, sent out by the Committee of Surveillance to all the Departments, expressing approval of the Massacres and exhorting
them to follow the noble example of Paris. Michelet and
Mortimer-Ternaux would have it that Marat printed this
letter and affixed the signatures of the other eight members
of the Committee without authority, but they adduce no
proof of their assertions; Ternaux, indeed, admits that he
himself never saw the original circular on which alone the
signatures were in writing. Braesch, who has made an in-
tensive study of the *Commune de Août 1792*, is of the opinion
that, though some of Marat's colleagues made such an accusation long after the fact, their avowals are only a belated
attempt to shift the onus of an unpopular act upon a deceased
scapegoat. The truth is that in the days immediately following the September Massacres, the reaction to them in
France was not in any degree as unfavorable as it later became.
Even in the best quarters they were looked upon as a regret-
table but natural explosion of popular feeling against those

who had incurred the hatred of the people.   Both Roland and
Danton felt that they were inevitable and almost necessary
in view of the circumstances in which Paris then was placed.
Each had neglected to exert his influence, whether as a private
individual, as a leader of a party, or as a public official, to
prevent bloodshed.   Roland publicly announced that he was
disposed "to draw a veil" over the entire matter.   Marat
himself kept justifying it as late as January and February
1793—indeed, even boasted of it.   In view of this it would
be difficult to maintain, as Jaurès does, that Marat gradually
recoiled from the responsibility for the Massacres and, in a
series of successive declarations, attempted to shift the blame
more and more on others' shoulders.   Whatever part he had
in that tragedy that can be definitely proved against him,
he never denied.   For to him the events of September 2–5,
1792 were a part of the insurrectionary measures that the
exigencies of the Revolution required.   Had he played a
greater rôle, he was the type of person that would have gloried
in it rather than concealed it.   That he was a member of
the group that was more culpable than any other can not be
denied.   But it can not be proved that he deliberately made
the plans and executed them.   The wide area of the Massacres, the apathy of the authorities whose duty it was to
preserve order, the general feeling of comparative indifference
after their occurrence—all tend to suggest that they were one
of those spontaneous uprisings that in times of revolution
need no special instigation from any popular leader.   Even
Braesch, who, of all the historians of these hectic days, has
the most capably maintained that the Massacres were carefully planned by the Committee of Surveillance, is able
to adduce no stronger argument than that certain of the
"executioners" were paid by the General Council of the Commune *the day after* the execution had started and then only
at the behest of the Sections.   It was only when the Mas-

sacres had receded into the past that for political reasons the
necessity for a scapegoat was felt and then it was discovered
that Marat was the likeliest quarry. Recent investigation
seems to indicate that Danton would have made a better one.

In the meantime Marat had been acting as secretary of
the Electoral Assembly of Paris and at the same time he had
been electioneering for himself, among others of Jacobin sympathies, as one of the candidates for the position of deputy
from the capital to the Convention and campaigning against
several pronounced Brissotins. He was supported by the
Jacobin Club, the *Révolutions de Paris*, Robespierre, and
several other important organizations and individuals, while
he was attacked by the Girondins, who had felt the bitterness of his tongue. On September 9, Marat was elected
one of the twenty-four Paris deputies by a vote of four
hundred and twenty out of a possible seven hundred and fifty-
eight, against twenty other candidates on the same ballot.
Priestley, the English chemist and philosopher, came second
with one hundred and one votes. Marat also received consideration on previous ballots. He was the seventh of the
Paris delegation to be elected, having been preceded only by
very well-known figures—Robespierre, Danton, Callot d'Her-
bois, Manuel, Billaud-Varennes, and Camille Desmoulins.
The friendship of Marat for the people was now being
reciprocated. His influence upon the citizens of Paris may
be estimated from the fact that not one of the candidates
whom he had opposed during the campaign he had conducted
in his columns was elected to represent the capital in the
Convention.

Thus it happened that Marat, though not yet a republican
himself, was a member of the National Convention, which on
September 22, 1792, made France a republic by acclamation.
If Marat was present at the opening sessions of the Con-

vention, he took no part in them. Nor did he commit himself for several days after the decrees of September 21–22, which abolished royalty and indirectly established the Republic. His paper did not appear again until September 25 and then was issued, not as the *Ami du Peuple*, but with the surprising title of the *Journal de la République française*. This was Marat's tacit acceptance of the Republic. In the first number, whether because he thought the creation of the Republic rendered strenuous measures unnecessary, or because he was weary of his fruitless labors, or because he feared to continue in his unpopular course, he announced a new policy for his journal:

> I am ready to take the means judged efficacious by the defenders of the people; I must march with them.

The second issue (September 26, 1792) gave an account of the session of the Convention on September 22, at which the Republic had been created, but made no comments, either adverse or favorable, regarding it. Marat seems to have accepted the Republic as a matter of course, now that it was a *fait accompli*, but certainly he had done nothing to bring it about.

Even now, however, his surrender was not unconditional. The Republic, he held, was weak; the French were not good republicans; they were not born for liberty. The words *République française* evidently struck no chord of sentiment within him; he preferred the words *la patrie* on the buttons of the army uniform. Moreover, he feared that as long as Louis XVI remained alive he would be the object of repeated conspiracies with which the Republic would be unable to cope. He therefore refused to believe in the Republic until Louis' head was severed from his shoulders. His aim, like Robespierre's, consequently, was to get rid of Louis in as quick

and expedient a manner as possible. His position with regard
to the entire problem of the trial of the King is completely
set forth in several issues of his journal. Some of these were
originally intended as speeches to the Convention and are to
be found in the minutes of that body's proceedings, although
he never had an opportunity to deliver them. In these addresses he argued that the Constitution of 1791, even though
it was a bad document to go by, since it had been drawn up
by a cabal of conspirators of whom the King had been the
leader and ought soon to be replaced by another framed by
the Convention itself, nevertheless provided for the punishment of Louis for treachery. For it stated definitely that the
monarch was to be regarded as having abdicated at the moment that he began to conspire against the country. Since
Louis had been in conspiracy with the enemies of France
long before August 10, he was now but a private citizen and
entitled to consideration only as such. Furthermore, there
was a higher law than the Constitution of 1791—the welfare
of the people—that must be borne in mind at this juncture.
Louis must therefore be tried by the Convention. And there
must be no referendum of the decision to the people, because
to consult the popular wish would be to cause a great loss
of time, encourage disorders, and prolong Louis' life and the
danger to the Republic. The penalty that the King must
pay ought to be execution, to be carried out with the least
possible delay. To insure a speedy conclusion of the trial,
Marat wished the number of charges against the former King
to be limited to as few as possible; indeed, his part in the
struggle of August 10, 1792, of which there was unimpeach-
able evidence, alone would suffice. Fearing that a certain
clique in the Convention was scheming to save Louis if possible or at least to delay his execution, Marat urged that the
vote on the decision be by roll-call and in writing upon special
registers. When the voting on the fate of the unfortunate

Bourbon finally took place (January 15-19, 1793) Marat voiced the opinion that the former King was guilty of treason, that no appeal to the people from the Convention should be permitted, that the death sentence should be imposed, and that execution should take place within twenty-four hours. Though for a moment the admirable conduct of Louis throughout his ordeal won favorable comment even from Marat, from the very first the Friend of the People had allowed no sentiment of sympathy or mercy to enter into the matter. The entire trial and execution of the unhappy Capet had been for him simply another necessary revolutionary measure. He summed up his attitude in a short declaration to the Convention, when he voted for the death of Louis:

> Gentlemen, you have decreed the Republic, but the Republic is only a house of cards until the head of the tyrant falls under the axe of the law.

Only when the quondam monarch was dead, and not until then, did Marat cry, "I believe in the Republic at last!" He repeated this profession three days later; and so complete was his conversion that he now began to believe that all of France had lost its love of royalty. To be sure, at about this time he put out a French edition of his *Chains of Slavery*, which contained the now no longer fashionable credo that democracy was best fitted for small states. But the book was known to have been written long before France had become a republic and therefore was not to be regarded as an attack upon the new government. When, after some months, the Constitution of 1793, which created the Republic one and indivisible was finally completed and accepted, though never applied, Marat greeted it with enthusiasm. He declared it to be "a monument of popularity and virtue," although, as Aulard has shown, it was not essentially different from the proposal of the Girondin committee which Marat had lashed scornfully.[1]

Marat's acceptance of the Republic required, of course, a change in his attitude toward the dictatorship. Beginning with his *Nouveau Marche*, the editorial in the first number of his *Journal de la République française* (September 25, 1792), in which he had announced that he would adopt a more moderate policy, he alluded to his stand on the dictatorship in an apologetic strain. Thereafter his change of attitude became more manifest. Both on the floor of the Convention and in his paper, he spoke of it as of a thing of the past, as of something he had once advised with the sincerest intentions, but now no longer deemed desirable. In a statement on November 8, 1792, he even admitted, though somewhat reluctantly, that there was a possibility of his having been mistaken—a tremendous admission for him. On November 9 his tone was somewhat more defiant though still apologetic. But on December 25, he expressed his fear that

> the enormous waste of the officials of the new regime, the alarming perfidy of the traitors who command the armies of the Republic, the excessive misery of the people, and the disorders of fearful anarchy carried to its worst will force the nation to renounce democracy in order to give itself a chief, if the Convention does not rise to the level of its important functions.

However, when berated that very day in the Convention on account of this assertion, he explained that it had been meant merely to rouse the Convention to action by pointing out the dire consequences awaiting further neglect of duty; nothing came of it. One of the rare bits of humor to be found in the pages of Marat's journals appeared on January 26, when

---

[1] The remarks that follow in this chapter lap over chronologically into the phases of Marat's career to be discussed in the next. It is advisable, however, to continue here the discussion of the effect of the death of the King upon Marat's dictatorship policy.

he announced ironically that the execution of Louis Capet had so shaken all thrones that he himself was prepared to abdicate the dictatorial crown that his enemies attributed to him. The dictatorship policy was now apparently relegated to the scrapheap.

Marat found a substitute for it in the Committees of General Security and Public Safety that the crises of March and April 1793 were to give birth to. He realized very clearly that a revolutionary government must have a strong executive. If the idea of a single dictator met with overwhelming unpopularity, then at least, he probably reasoned, let there be a committee of dictators—which was but a dictatorship program disguised to deceive his enemies. Indeed, he went so far as to demand that the administration of the War Department be put into the hands of a committee, because the work was too much for one man. It is significant also that in times of crises, as when Dumouriez threatened to march upon Paris and purge the Convention, Marat, instead of clamoring for a dictator, as he once undoubtedly would have done, now demanded that a Committee of Public Safety be created. All the effort that he had formerly exerted to make popular insurrections under a dictator possible was now devoted to rendering efficient these new revolutionary bodies. He desired that their membership should be small and of tried patriots, and that they be enabled to take decisive action against foreign and internal enemies, regardless of position or rank.

On April 20, 1793, at a time when he had been obliged once more and for the last time to go into hiding from the police, his bitterness swept away all the good sense that he had generally applied to the punishment of crime. Although he had spoken in his *Plan de législation criminelle* and elsewhere of the necessity of penalties being in proportion to the crimes committed, he now advocated, together with the erec-

tion of two committees—one of general defense and the other
of general security,—the enactment of three laws: firstly, all
ci-devants, former monks and officials of the Ancient Regime
shall be obliged to wear their old costumes and shall not be
permitted to hold office under the Republic or to appear in
popular assemblies or meet in greater numbers than three,
under penalty of death; secondly, every public functionary
who has conspired against the country shall be punished by
death; thirdly, every civil official guilty of embezzlement
shall lose his right ear, every military official guilty of evil
intentions his two thumbs, and every henchman of the former
King or any officer who, having been driven out of one army
corps for lack of discipline, shall have enlisted in another,
his two thumbs also. But he never referred to this Draconic
proposal again, and it is likely that he had announced such a
frightful program only to emphasize the need for vesting ter-
roristic powers in the hands of the new committees. When
he saw in these committees men whom he utterly distrusted,
he protested vehemently, even in his last days, when illness
limited his protests to feeble bursts of indignation in his
journal. The very last number that he edited, which appeared on the day after his death, argued for a reorganization
of the Committee of Public Safety for the sake of greater
vigor in its activities. How completely he had changed his
policy—at least to outward appearances—is to be gathered
from his refuting the contention that the Committee of Public Safety would eventually result in a dictatorship—a contention which at one time would have been his principal
argument in favor of any plan.

So thoroughly had Marat lived down his reputation as the
chief and only adherent of the dictatorship that from December 1792 until April 12, 1793, although, as we shall see, he
was frequently the object of the attacks of the Girondins in
the Convention, the charge—so often made before December

1792—of having agitated for a tribunate found no place in them. The details of these attacks will be discussed later, but it is important to note here that, when it was decided to hail Marat before the Revolutionary Tribunal, the report of the committee which drew up the charges against him made no mention of his having preached in favor of a dictatorship, although the introductory statement of the chairman indicated that that had not entirely escaped attention. It was only as an afterthought, on the suggestion of La Revellière-Lepaux, that it was made one of the grounds of accusation against him.[1]

When brought to trial, Marat replied to this charge with an almost categorical denial. Inasmuch as the act of accusation had been limited to the issues of the *Journal de la République française*, this was actually true, since, from the time the *Ami du Peuple* had become the *Journal de la République française*, Marat seemed definitely to have repudiated the dictatorship policy. He now maintained that such an accusation could not seriously have been made against him, the undying enemy of tyrants and kings, the most ardent rebel against all arbitrary powers. And some weeks later, with almost his last breath, he spoke ironically of "the Dictator Marat . . . , a poor devil who would give all the dignities of the earth for a few days of health, but always a hundred times more occupied with the misfortunes of the people than with his own illness."

Despite all of these denials by implication, assertion, and act, there is nevertheless some reason to believe that even now Marat had not wholly given up his faith in the necessity and efficacy of the dictator. Even in November 1792, when he was most intent upon ridding himself of the stigma of having proposed such a policy, he spoke of "chiefs of whom

[1] Archives parlementaires, LXVII, April 13, 1792, pp. 24–75; LXVIII, April 20, 1793, p. 29 *et seq.* Both the *Acte d'accusation contre Marat* and the *Appel nominal sur la question: Y-a-t-il lieu à accusation contre Marat* were printed separately by the order of the Convention.

the people always have need in times of revolution to direct their terrible movements." On February 8, 1793, he pointed out that the weakness of democratic government lay in its inefficiency in times of crisis. In fact, on the occasion of one of those crises of which he was in constant dread—the fall of the Girondins,—Marat for the moment again felt the need of a dictator to lead a popular insurrection. On May 31, 1793, he was overheard to voice the desire that the people might have such a dictator. He was denounced accordingly by Billaud-Varennes and Robert at the Society of the Jacobins. On June 3, in an address to the Society, he confessed that he had expressed such a wish to representatives of several sections of Paris who had come to ask his advice. He insisted, however, that by dictator he meant "a guide, a chief, and not a master" and that "these words are not synonymous." In a subsequent letter to the Jacobins on June 20, 1793, he again admitted having asked for a dictator on May 31, but claimed to have added, when a nearby Girondin appeared to have been shocked:

> A chief in my language is not a master: no one has more horror of a master than I. But in times of actual crisis, I want chiefs to direct the operations of the people in order that they may take no false steps and that their efforts may not be futile.

The Jacobins, on the whole, were friendly to Marat. They regarded his explanation as sufficient and ordered his letter to be printed and circulated. It was not necessary for him to conceal his true feelings in addressing them to the same extent as in the Convention or in public utterances. The entire episode leads to the suspicion that Marat had repudiated his dictatorship doctrine partially, to be sure, because of his belief in the Republic, but also because of a desire to avoid further attacks on that score. Perhaps, had he lived long enough and had an acute crisis occurred, he might again have urged the dictatorship. The possibility of such a contingency, however, was precluded by his sudden death about three weeks after the letter just quoted was written.

Marat's plan for a dictatorship is another case in which his bark was worse than his bite. After all, he merely desired to set himself up for a few days as the leader of the Revolution until the results he hoped for should be achieved. Any man who believed himself capable of such a position would probably have demanded the same distinction, if he had been at all able to make his demand heard. In simple words, what Marat was trying to say was, "Put me in a position to arrange matters, and in a few days everything will be all right." Such a desire may be vain and ambitious; but it is quite intelligible and undeserving of the condemnation that it has brought upon Marat. Mounier, Mirabeau, Danton and Robespierre might very well have given voice to the same thought without meeting with the same chorus of protest. If any of them had done so, however, it must be admitted that his language would have been much more subtle than Marat's.

In short, what distinguished Marat from these others was not so much his inordinate ambition as his lack of conventional restraint upon it; not so much his political philosophy (like theirs, it was borrowed largely from Rousseau and Montesquieu) as the violence and candor of the language in which it was propounded. To understand the reason for this, it must be remembered that the change of mind that Marat underwent was in itself a severe mental struggle such as few revolutionary figures had been called upon to undergo—a change from perfectly bourgeois notions at the beginning of his revolutionary career to the ideals of an aspirant for a dictatorship over the Paris populace, brought about through "despair at seeing the normal plan of the Revolution disrupted by the stupidity of the moderate bourgeoisie."

Nor must it be forgotten that, if his language was more truc-
ulent than that of other disciples of Rousseau—Danton and
Robespierre, for instance,—they had never had to lie hidden
in subterranean refuges, had never lost their fortunes, had
never suffered from foul diseases, because of their devotion
to the revolutionary ideal.   This suffering may not justify
Marat's cruelty and extreme violence, but it at least helps
to explain it.   And, to adapt Bagehot's oft-quoted epigram,
the difficulty in historical appreciation is not in seeing the
merits and demerits of a political career, but in grasping the
problems that had to be confronted during that career.

CHAPTER V

WHEN, on September 20, 1792, the National Convention met at the Manège in Paris, it was found to be divided into three distinct parties. The radicals of the former Legislative Assembly—the Brissotins and the Girondins, representing the departments of the Gironde and its neighbors—now sat upon the Right. The position on the Left had been inherited by the deputies from Paris and their adherents, who became known, at first, as the Jacobins, because many of them were members of the Jacobin Club, and, later, as the Mountain, because their seats were more elevated than the others; they represented the opinions of their Paris constituencies. Neither of these two factions controlled a majority of the Convention, but their importance far exceeded their number because the one could boast of such leaders as Vergniaud, Brissot, and Roland, and the other Robespierre and Marat. The majority of the Convention sat in the Centre and had no pronounced sympathies with either faction. Consequently their support was problematical. Neither the Mountain nor the Gironde could accomplish anything against the other, although the antagonism between them was great, without the aid of a sufficient number of the members of the Marsh or Plain, as the Centre party was named. At first the Girondins had enough influence over the Marsh to be the dominant element in the Convention, though not so dominant as to be able to overwhelm the Jacobin opposition completely. Indeed, at first the Centre endeavored to act as a mediator between the two parties. One of its leaders, the Prussian Anacharsis Cloots, wrote a brochure entitled *Ni Marat ni Roland*, a plea for the ending of factious strife and for co-operation in the cause of Liberty. But his advice went unheeded. And so, while the fate of the Republic was in jeopardy, both in domestic and in foreign warfare, much valuable time was squandered by the deputies of the people in partisan squabbles.

Marat soon became a storm-centre. With the monarchy abolished and the King dead, he was now certain that the single obstacle in the way of the establishment of a government such as he wished—a government maintained for the benefit of the great mass of the common people by representatives of their own choosing—was the Girondins. They now stepped into the rôle of villains in the drama that had formerly been occupied in his suspicious mind variously by the Constituent Assembly, the Constitution of 1791, and the late King; they were the rallying-point of the counter-revolution.

Even as recent students of the French Revolution as Kropotkin and Mathiez find it possible to share Marat's feelings in this respect, to maintain that the issue between the Girondins and the Jacobins of the Mountain was the ever-prevalent one of bourgeois property-holders against radical reformers bent upon political and social equality.[1] Aulard, on the other

---

[1] Mathiez has recently presented a convenient summary of his views (Third Lecture on *La Convention* in the *Revue des Cours et Conferences*, 1923, pp. 1201-1202): "Can it be said, as has lightly been asserted, that there was no disagreement between Girondins and Montagnards on principle, that they were separated from each other only by personal rivalries and by their conceptions of the rôle that the capital ought to play in the direction of public affairs? Nothing could be more inexact. Between the Girondins and the Montagnards the conflict was profound. It was almost a class conflict. The Girondins, as Daunou remarked, comprised a great number of property-holders and citizens; they had the feeling for social hierarchies that they wanted preserved and strengthened. They experienced an instinctive dislike for the coarse and un-cultured people. . . . The Montagnards, on the contrary, represented the lower classes, those who suffered from the crisis of the war, those who had overturned

hand, claims that there was no precise disagreement on social or political questions between the Jacobins and the Girondins save the contention regarding the predominance of Paris over the Departments.   In either case, at a time when feeling ran constantly at fever heat and death was fast becoming the penalty for failure, the elements of personal dislikes and rival ambitions must not be discounted.   For contemporary politicians, no less than for later historians, the entire matter was extremely complex and difficult to understand.   When a man as level-headed as Barère, in addressing the Convention (March 18, 1793), could draw a distinction between the two parties on the grounds that the one believed the Revolution was achieved while the other insisted there was much yet to be accomplished, it is not surprising that one as hot-headed as Marat should have regarded the Girondins as reactionaries. To explain his attitude toward the Girondins it is necessary to go back as far as the year 1791, when they first became recognized as a definite political organization.

If Marat eventually came to believe that the struggle with the Gironde was a clear-cut one of patriots against counter-revolutionaries, it was not without a process of more or less conscious rationalization that it became possible for him to do so.   In the beginning, when, indeed, the Girondins were among the most stalwart in the Jacobin Club, he had drawn no such distinction between them and the Paris deputation to the Legislative Assembly.   In that short-lived organization, the man who found most favor in his esteem was Isnard, later one of the most hated of Girondins; and although Marat did not share the universal enthusiasm for Pétion when that

the throne, those who had elevated themselves to political rights by insurrection. . . . The Girondins were detested not only in Paris, the city which had defied and repudiated them, but the city which first had created that policy of public safety, which had formulated and put into practice the exceptional and dictatorial measures for which the class they represented was forcibly to pay the expenses."

popular Constituent became mayor of Paris, nevertheless the issues of the *Ami du Peuple* contained expressions of approval of him that were unusual for Marat. When the representatives of both Paris and the Gironde supported the project, initiated in June 1792, to station twenty thousand men in a camp near Paris, a war measure which Marat interpreted as an attempt to intimidate the capital, he denounced indiscriminately "the disloyal deputies of the people, such as those of Paris and of the Gironde." All this, however, was before a recognized Girondin or Brissotin faction definitely existed. When such a party came into being, Marat was not slow in giving vent to his antipathy.

It was largely due to Marat's hostility to Brissot, who was the acknowledged leader of the Girondins in the Legislative Assembly, that this feeling of opposition arose. Until the beginning of 1790 Brissot and Marat had been good friends personally and politically. Then Marat began to suspect that Brissot's journal, *Le Patriote Français*, was sold to royalist interests, and this suspicion, though it had no substantial basis in fact, steadily gained strength as it grew older. The declaration of war against Austria, which Brissot and his followers had heartily endorsed and Marat had bitterly opposed, served only to widen the breach. The Jacobin Club had split into two factions upon the issue of war with Austria. The majority at first supported Brissot, but a staunch minority followed the leadership of Robespierre, who was fearful of the outcome of hostilities; and Marat was one of this minority. The breach, once made, widened quickly. Marat began regularly to attack the Girondins and they, in turn, launched against him the decree of accusation of May 3, 1792, which we have already seen him escape by careful hiding. In this way, by the time the Legislative Assembly gave way to the National Convention, the deputies of the Gironde and the Bouches-du-Rhone had become Marat's newest *bête noire*.

In the same placards in which he advocated the election of Danton, Robespierre, Fréron, Billaud-Varennes, Camille Desmoulins, and other Jacobins, he asked for the rejection of Brissot, Vergniaud, Lasource, Guadet, Louvet, Condorcet, and others of their political affiliations. Nor were his enemies silent regarding him; they replied to each of his denunciations in kind in the journals that they owned or controlled.[1]

War between Marat and the Gironde was thus practically declared before the opening of the National Convention. Soon after the first ardor of the creation of the Republic had passed, the strife between the Mountain and the Gironde began. On September 25, the entire Paris delegation was accused by Lasource of having sought a dictator for France. Robespierre, Danton, and Panis denied the charge, claiming to have had no cognizance of Marat's plans. Marat was left to face his enemies alone.

"I demand the floor," he cried.

Violent murmurs, mingled with heated and indignant cries of "Get down from the tribune!" arose on all sides. Delacroix, however, insisted that in all fairness Marat ought to be heard, and Marat was allowed to ascend the tribune.

"Have I then in this Assembly," he began, "a great number of personal enemies?"

"All! All!" the entire Convention is reported to have answered, rising to its feet in its indignation.

"If I have in this Assembly a great number of enemies, I appeal to their sense of shame not to oppose with vain clamor, shouts, and threats a man who has devoted himself to the country, and to their own welfare. It is not by threats and outrages that an accused man is convinced that he is culpable. It is not by crying out against a defender of the people that he

---

[1] *Marat . . . aux Amis de la Patrie,* in Chevremont, *Placards,* dated by Chevremont August 5, 1792, but really of September 5. See Charavay, *Assemblées électorales de Paris,* III, p. xix, fn. 2.

can be shown that he is a criminal. Let them listen to me a moment in silence. I will not abuse their patience."

And he went on in a truly eloquent speech to explain what a limited interpretation he put upon the term *dictator*, to exculpate Danton and Robespierre from the charge of having conspired with him, to assure the Convention of the utmost sincerity of his intentions and of the unselfish patriotism of his motives, and to plead for a surcease of discord and for unison of action in the face of the Republic's numerous enemies. In order to prove his earnestness in asking for peace within the Convention, he caused to be read the issue of his *Journal de la République française*, which had made its maiden appearance that day, containing his declaration that he would begin a *nouveau marche* and pursue a more moderate policy thenceforth. For a moment the matter seemed closed, when Vergniaud arose and called the attention of the assembly to the fact that Marat was still under the taint of the decrees of outlawry passed against him by the defunct Châtelet and the Legislative Assembly. He also took the occasion to read the letter of September 3 that Marat and the other members of the Committee of Police and Surveillance had written to the Departments in approbation of the September Massacres. Cries of *"A l'Abbaye!"* and *"Decret d'accusation!"* went up. And in the uproar Marat defiantly retorted that he gloried in both the outlawry and the letter. Finally some cooler deputies moved for the order of the day and the Convention passed on to its regular business. After the storm had blown over, Marat, drawing a pistol from his belt, placed it to his temple and shouted that if the decree of accusation had been carried against him, he would have blown out his brains there and then. He himself, with his complete lack of sense of humor, probably thought he meant every word of what he said. At any rate with the danger already passed, it was an effective and, on the whole, safe gesture to make. The Convention passed on to the order of the day without taking any definite action in the matter.

This was the first pitched battle between the two opposing factions and it ended without a conclusive decision. Consequently neither the Girondins nor Marat were anxious to keep the peace for any length of time. The attack upon Marat was resumed on October 4, but again it came to naught. On October 24, Barbaroux accused Marat of courting favor with some Marseillais troops in Paris for his own ends and of demanding 200,000 heads. Both of these charges, without denying either directly, Marat explained away. As he left the tribune and took his seat again, Camille Desmoulins was heard to say to him, "You are two centuries ahead of your time." And Camille was too serious-minded a youth to be a humorist! Barbaroux's denunciation was sent to the Committee of Surveillance and Legislation of the Convention for consideration and report. Five days later, in a tirade directed against Marat, Robespierre, and the Jacobins in general, Louvet de Couvrai denounced the former for having urged insurrection, particularly the September Massacres, and for having sponsored the dictatorship project. After another long and tumultuous discussion, Louvet's speech was ordered printed and circulated and the matter submitted to the Committee of General Security for consideration. There it was allowed to smoulder.

These repeated attacks in the Convention had the effect of rousing some of the troops in Paris to action. They went about the streets, shouting against Marat, Danton, and Robespierre, invading even the District of the Cordeliers in their zeal to do violence to the objects of their wrath. Marat again was forced to seek refuge in hiding and appealed to the Society of the Jacobins for its protection. At the same time a petition for the expulsion of Marat from the Convention was presented to that body, though it was not acted upon.

Meanwhile the conduct of Philippe Égalité, the former Duc d'Orleans, came under suspicion and each party pretended to believe that the other was in league with him. In order to contradict the implication that he had meant Orleans for the dictatorship, Marat made the declaration in his journal (*Journal*, no. 84, December 25, 1792) that even if the Convention should allow the condition of France to become worse than it already was and the people therefore were to demand a dictator, Orleans would be the last person whom he would support for that office. This was interpreted by his enemies as an attack upon the Convention as well as a renewal of his demand for a dictator, and on December 25, he was assailed on these grounds. But again (as we have already seen) he was able to make satisfactory explanations.

During all this period the fate of Louis XVI was under consideration. The Girondins were on the whole in favor of moderation toward the King, and it was among their number that were to be found the chief supporters of the ideas of referring the sentence of the King to the people, of punishment by exile or life imprisonment rather than death, and, these lenitive measures failing, of delay in the execution of the capital penalty. In all this Marat could see only conspiracy and treason. Were not the Girondins allied with the odious arch-conspirator Roland? Madame Roland wished "impartial posterity" to think that Marat's opposition to her husband was due to his having disregarded Marat's requests for aid from the funds put at the disposal of the Minister of the Interior to help needy writers. To be sure, Marat did ask for such aid, but if Madame Roland's implication is true at all, it is true only in part, for the fact that Roland had formerly been a minister of the fallen tyrant was alone sufficient to condemn him in Marat's judgment. Moreover, had not many of the Girondins been members of the perfidious Constituent and Legislative Assemblies? It was all completely manifest to him.   If the King was obliged at his trial to tell all he knew regarding his conspiracies, he would necessarily implicate some of the Girondins.   It was natural, therefore, that they as a group should favor leniency toward the quondam monarch and be intent upon delaying the completion of his trial as long as possible.   For that reason they had invented the scheme of appealing to the people and, in addition, were planning to have the Convention transferred from Paris to some other city.   He even claimed that the Girondins were deliberately fomenting tumult in Paris in order to have better grounds for the removal of the Convention; and when certain deputies complained that they had been threatened with violence unless they voted for the death of Louis, Marat announced that he considered that, too, part of the plot to discredit the capital.   This accusation, made two days before the vote on the fate of the King (January 16, 1793), threatened for a moment to distract the attention of the Convention from Louis XVI and concentrate it upon Marat.   But the incipient attack was squelched by vigorous addresses of Danton, Robespierre, and Marat, and the trial of the ex-monarch went on. In number after number of the *Journal de la République française* as well as in speeches from the floor of the Convention, Marat continued to arraign the *faction Roland* as royalists devoted to the tyrant.   Even the final decision to execute the King and its enforcement put no end to these denunciations.

The reply of the Girondins, of course, was to publish broadcast similar attacks upon Marat and his colleagues.   Brissot, Roland, Barbaroux, Condorcet, and others used their literary powers to pen bitter diatribes against him.   Kersaint resigned from the Convention after the trial of the King had come to a close, giving as his reason that he "could no longer sit in an assembly in which blood-thirsty men dominated, in an assembly where Marat triumphed over Pétion!"   The Girondins, however, having for the time being a sufficient influence over the Marsh to command a majority in the Convention, preferred, whenever an opportunity was presented, to attack Marat on the floor of the Convention rather than to resort exclusively to the press, in the hopes of securing a decree of accusation against him.

The concentration of attention which the last days of the trial of Louis had demanded had temporarily halted the clashes with Marat. Except for the feeble attempt on January 16, they were not renewed until February 26. There had been a food riot in Paris on the previous day, and Marat's enemies tried to place the responsibility for it upon him. His issue of February 25 had informed the starving Paris populace that in some countries, when famine conditions prevailed, the people obtained their food from the shops by force. It has been shown that this statement actually came too late to have influenced the riot in any way. This was not the first time, however, that Marat had spoken in such tones; and that his influence did play some part in the events of February 25 is shown by the leadership assumed by Jacques Roux, a notorious Constitutional priest and a great admirer of Marat, who had arrogated to himself the title of *the Marat of the Commune.* Evidently neither Marat nor his enemies knew whether he had incited the riot or not; but on the following day Salle charged him with the responsibility for it. Marat's defense was to equivocate, claiming that his remarks could not have been construed as an incitation to riot, as they were only a statement of what was true in other countries. Once more the attack halted. This time it was not to be renewed until the Girondins were ready for a supreme effort.

Indeed, in the period during which the Convention discussed the erection of a Revolutionary Tribunal with extraordinary powers to suppress counter-revolution (March 8–13, 1793), Marat tried to bring to an end the internecine struggle between the two factions. Although he had taken no part in the debates upon the proposed tribunal, nevertheless, on the 10th of March, the day after the creation of the tribunal had been decreed and when the details of its construction were still under discussion, as he left the hall, the same crowd that had just insulted the Girondins Pétion and Beurnonville was reported by Vergniaud and others to have carried Marat in triumph from the session.   Perhaps Marat felt that he could therefore afford to be magnanimous.   At any rate, if we are to believe his own repeated declaration, he had preached peace at the Cordeliers and urged the patriotic societies to protect all members of the Convention.   On March 12, when petitioners from the Section Poissonière attacked Dumouriez and the leaders of the Girondins, Marat, despite the taunts hurled at him as he spoke, insisted that the petitioners were suborned by aristocrats in the hope of dividing the Convention.   Dumouriez, he said, is necessary for the success of the army.   "And I, who do not love the *hommes d'état*, declare that rather than let any attack against them succeed, I will make a rampart of my body for them, at the same time that I will defend it against their machinations."   He demanded and received action against Fournier, called "the American," who had been brazenly blatant in his threats against various celebrities of the Convention.   But even as Marat spoke in this vein, he denounced the Girondins for intending to rise against the patriots in the Convention as soon as the deputies on mission had departed and to move the Convention to some aristocratic city; and for a good part of the remainder of the session of March 12, Lasource and he tilted away at each other verbally. It was quite clear by this time that an understanding between the two factions was impossible.

Since his first appearance in the Convention, Marat had been treated with the utmost discourtesy and contempt by the Right.   About the only proposals that he ever made that were not bitterly contested or jeered were on December 13,

1792, when he moved that the troops who had been at the front for a long time should be replaced by those stationed in Paris, and on March 25 and 29, 1793, when he advocated the sequestration of pleasure horses for military purposes. On other occasions his deportment invited a turbulent reception. Whenever he spoke, it was to incriminate someone or denounce something. He was constantly bobbing up to demand the floor on some point of order or in the name of public safety, or shouting out without having obtained the floor. At first he was greeted with bursts of laughter, but as time went on, the cries of *"A l'Abbaye!"* and *"Decret d'accusation!"* became more frequent. Whenever there was a Girondin chairman of the Convention, he had great difficulty in getting permission to speak. He claimed that on one occasion (December 15, 1792) he tried for an hour to be heard; the Convention in a special vote finally decided not to hear him. Boileau once demanded that "whenever Marat speaks at this tribune, it be purified immediately." And one day (February 21, 1793) he and Génissieu actually came to blows when both attempted to speak from the tribune at the same time; Marat was bustled off the platform amid cries of *"A l'Abbaye!"* Upon his continued insistence, a vote of censure was taken, and he was refused permission to speak by a large majority. Marat later claimed that he had deliberately created this disturbance in order to filibuster, hoping to prevent the defeat of a proposal then before the Convention to allow soldiers to name their own officers. On a later occasion he was ushered off the tribune by one of the official ushers of the Convention (April 12, 1793).

Naturally enough, Marat's condemnation of the Girondins became more acrid with such treatment. His conviction remained firm that their guilty associations with Louis XVI had dictated their moderate attitude in connection with his trial. He also made frequent use of the popular notion that the

Girondins were scheming to divide France up into numerous federated republics, although he later admitted (*Publiciste de la République française*, no. 201, May 24, 1793) that he really did not believe that they advocated such a policy. He continued to maintain that they were hiring ruffians to create disturbances so as to arouse the Departments against Paris. Furthermore, Marat could see no reason for the desire of a certain group of the Girondins to turn the war, which had so far been of a defensive character, into an offensive war. For with the proselytizing fervor that characterizes revolutionists, the Convention had decreed, on November 19, 1792, that the French people would "accord fraternity and assistance to all peoples who shall wish to recover their liberty" and on December 15 that it would "treat as enemies the people who, refusing liberty and equality, or renouncing them, may wish to preserve, recall, or treat with the prince and the privileged castes." Marat realized that such decrees were aggressive propaganda and that up to that moment the aggressions of France had gained for her more enemies than friends. As early as December 1792 he recognized that the cause of England's hostility to France was not her opposition to the popular movements of August 10 or September 2–5, or her King's sympathy for Louis XVI so much as her misgivings that France might open the Scheldt River to commerce; and he declared that he had opposed the union of Savoy with France in November of that year for fear of creating a similar feeling of uneasiness among other European powers. All these policies, whether exclusively Girondin or not, redounded in his opinion to their discredit.

As was to be expected, Marat opposed the plan for a constitution that the Girondins proposed. On October 11, 1792 a committee to attend to the drawing up of a new instrument of government had been appointed. It was made up entirely of members of the Gironde and the Plain. After the execu-

tion of Louis XVI, this committee was ready to report and
did so, on February 15, through its chairman Condorcet.
Marat naturally found its proposals highly objectionable: the
declaration of rights was obscure; it gave too much power
to the primary assemblies; it contained too many details in
providing for the organization of the legislature. Marat's
objections to this proposal for a constitution, combined with
the arguments against it made by other Montagnards, succeeded in delaying its acceptance until the overthrow of the
Girondins, which followed a few months later, when a new
committee, controlled by the Jacobins, was appointed.

Shortly after Condorcet's report, an address bewailing the
evils of the country and calling upon the people to guard
themselves against the inimical Gironde was issued by several
Paris deputies. Among the latter was, of course, Marat,
who also took care to have it printed in his journal (no. 129,
February 21, 1793). Marat's paper was a dangerous weapon
constantly aimed in the direction of the Girondins, who consequently took vigorous measures to have it suppressed. On
March 9 they succeeded in passing a law which required members of the Convention who edited newspapers or journals to
choose between their duties as legislators and journalists, the
performance of both at the same time becoming illegal.
While there were more journalists in the ranks of their own
party than among the Montagnards, the decree apparently was
intended especially for Marat. It was repealed very soon,
but while it remained in force, Marat coolly ignored it and
refused to give up his paper. He yielded, however, to the extent of changing its name. There could be no objections, of
course, to a deputy's reporting to his constituents, and so,
for a few issues, he called his journal *Observations à mes
commettans*. Occasionally, too, since apparently there was
some distinction to be drawn between a journalist and a pub-
licist, he employed the title *Publiciste de la Révolution fran-*

çaise. On April 4 Barère called the attention of the Convention to the fact that Marat was not obeying the law of March 9. A discussion arose, at the end of which the Girondins, probably in consideration of the importance to them of Condorcet's journal, consented to repeal the unenforced measure. Accordingly, with no. 164 of April 9, 1793, Marat's publication became definitely the *Publiciste de la Révolution française*—in every respect save for this slight change of title exactly like the former productions of its editor. With this title the journal continued without any serious interruptions until Marat's death. The last number appeared upon the day after his assassination. One of the earliest declarations of the newly named leaflet was made on March 21, 1793, in which the editor declared that until the *hommes d'état*, as he derisively called the Girondins, were dismissed from the Convention, he would "daily stamp upon their brows the seal of opprobrium." Skilled as he was in the art of invective, he was able to fulfill this threat without any seeming difficulty.

It was the defection of General Dumouriez that brought matters to a climax. In October 1792, Dumouriez had had two battalions of Paris volunteers, known by the appellations of *Mauconseil* and *le Républicain*, arrested and sent to Paris for imprisonment, on the charge of having killed four Prussian soldiers who had deserted to them. When Marat first heard the story, he suspected that it was not wholly true. He applied to the Committee of Military Affairs of the Convention and to the Department of War for more precise information, but could get no satisfaction. On the basis of some facts furnished him by one of his numerous correspondents, he began to believe that the four Prussian deserters whom the two battalions had assassinated were in reality French émigrés captured with arms in hand. Dumouriez himself soon came to Paris to attend a conference on the plans for the conquest of

Belgium. Marat, with two Jacobins as witnesses, sought to interview him. After a frantic search they found that he was being entertained at the home of Thalma, the actor, and decided to call upon him there. So, with his two companions, the slovenly Marat broke in upon a brilliant gathering in order to cross-examine the guest of honor. Dumouriez treated them curtly and refused to impart any more information than he had already put at the disposal of the Convention. This only increased Marat's suspicions. On October 17, he felt called upon to render a report of his investigations, denouncing the General for vilifying patriotic troops. Gradually further evidence corroborated the suspicion that the murdered men had been émigrés and not Prussian deserters; and finally Marat demanded of the Convention a decree of accusation against Chazot, the general who, subordinate to Dumouriez, had been in immediate command of the two guilty battalions. Dumouriez and Chazot were thereafter bitterly assailed in the pages of the *Journal de la République française*. On November 29, 1792, Marat declared his willingness to wager that before March 1793 Dumouriez would himself have emigrated, and he missed his guess by just a few days. Eventually the *Affaire de Dumouriez* ended with the acquittal of the two battalions.

The next step—though it was taken perhaps entirely without premeditation by Marat—was to make it appear that the Girondins were in conspiracy with Dumouriez. This process began in March 1793. It was comparatively easy for him to prove his point, since the Girondins had always supported the General. Marat remembered that Dumouriez had been called to the Ministry at the same time as Roland. Events fast precipitated a climax. In February Dumouriez had failed to take Maestricht and on March 18 he was defeated at Neerwinden. Perhaps he was already in conspiracy with the Austrians and the émigrés. At any rate, he had regarded the execution of Louis XVI as a grave mistake and was agitated by the radical measures of the extremists in the Convention. Furthermore, he had his own ambitious schemes for the reorganization of France, Belgium, and Holland. When his views became known, the Convention sent representatives to check him. These he imprisoned and turned over to the Austrians. He then sent a letter to the Convention threatening to march upon Paris, drive "the satellites of Marat and Robespierre" from the Convention, and turn the government over to the "sane majority of the Assembly." This was proof-positive of his treasonable relations with the Right in Marat's mind, and Marat did not delay in casting this new charge at his enemies. As we have seen, he now began his agitation for the concentration of authority in the hands of a Committee of Public Safety. At the same time he succeeded in securing the suppression of the Committee of Six that supervised the work of the Revolutionary Tribunal, claiming that since it was made up almost entirely of Girondins, it checked rather than expedited the work of that body.

On April 5, 1793, Dumouriez deserted, taking with him the young Égalité, son of the former Duke of Orleans. The Convention vented its emotions upon the father of the lad. As has been seen, Marat had now to face the charge of having been an Orleanist, an accusation that he in turn added to the many that he laid at the door of the Girondins. To put a halt to further imputations of such a nature, Marat proposed outlawing the entire Capetian house. When delay occurred in bringing this suggestion to a vote, he again saw in it proof of the royalist tendencies of the Girondin party.

The critical moment had now come when the Gironde must put forth its full strength to crush Marat or itself be crushed. The period immediately following the defection of Dumouriez seemed to them to be most opportune. About half of the deputies were away "on mission," and most of these were Montagnards. There is no evidence to show that the attack on Marat on April 12 was preconcerted, but it must have been obvious to individual Girondins that, if the ever recurrent offensive were to be resumed, there was more likelihood of a decree of accusation passing at this time than there ever had been before or was ever likely to be again. At any rate, Marat offered to his enemies a good reason for once more demanding such a decree. On April 5 he had become president of the Jacobin Club. That day the Jacobins drew up a circular letter attacking the generals of the army, the moderate faction of the Convention, and—particularly—Dumouriez, and urging the Departments to come to the defense of Paris. Marat, as president, had signed the declaration. On April 12, Guadet read it to the Convention, and immediately a clamor for a decree of accusation was set up on the Right. While the Friend of the People admitted that the principles of the document had his full endorsement, he protested that his signature to it was but a mere formality. Great hubbub was created in his favor in the Mountain and in the Galleries. But finally, on the motion of Lacroix, it was decreed that Marat be put in a state of arrest and a committee was appointed to report upon the grounds of his impeachment. The question was raised as to whether the arrest was to be in Marat's own home or in the Abbaye and was decided in favor of the latter arrangement. A warrant was made out immediately, but in the tumult it was not signed by the proper authorities. Taking advantage of this irregularity, Marat refused to allow himself to be made a prisoner. Surrounded by his friends in the Mountain, he made good his retreat before another warrant for his arrest could be formally executed. For the last time in his career Marat went into hiding again. His first step was to write a letter to the Convention, which was read at its next session, in which he declared that the decree launched against him was part of the treasonable conspiracy of the Girondins with Dumouriez and Orleans, and the beginning of a wholesale attack upon the Mountain.

The next day, the committee of the Convention which had been appointed to draw up the act of accusation gave its report through Delaunay the younger. It stated, as the chief complaints, that Marat had incited pillage, murder, and attacks upon the Convention, and quoted examples from his writings. La Revellière-Lepaux called attention to the fact that nothing had been said of the dictatorship policy of Marat, and the Committee took this suggestion under consideration. When the letter of the Jacobins of April 5, which had been the immediate cause of the decree against Marat on the previous day, was again read, a large number of Montagnards, led by Dubois-Crancé and David, melodramatically rose from their seats and signed their names to it also, thereby indicating their support of its contentions and of Marat. A vote was then taken on whether or not Marat was to be hailed before the recently established Revolutionary Tribunal. It was the first time since the vote on the death of Louis XVI that an *appel nominal* was taken—an honor not to be granted later to either Danton or Robespierre. From ten o'clock in the evening of April 13 until seven o'clock in the morning of the next day, the colleagues of the accused went, one by one, to the tribune and cast their votes with appropriate—and sometimes verbose—remarks. During those nine hours, all sorts of opinions about Marat, from accusations of downright insanity or homicidal disposition, on the one hand, to eulogies for the purest patriotism and the most unselfish devotion, on the other, were pronounced as the votes were recorded. As was to be expected, the voting, with but a few exceptions, was along strictly party lines. The final count, including a few votes later received by letter from absent deputies, was 226 for accusation, 93 against accusation, 374 on mission, 47 absent, 7 demanding adjournment, and 3 refusing to vote. Marat was thus the first deputy of the people to suffer from a recent decision to rescind the inviolability of the nation's representatives, who hitherto could not legally have been molested for their political activities.

On April 20, the Committee on the grounds for the indictment submitted its final report, which was ordered printed. The act of accusation was now amended so as to include Marat's having preached pillage and murder, having attempted to destroy the sovereignty of the people—or in other words having proposed a dictator,—and having urged the dissolution of the Convention. Documents in substantiation of each of these three contentions, consisting mainly of excerpts from his journals, were appended. Meanwhile, Marat, pleading ill-health, refused to surrender to the police. Despite the rigorous attempts to effect his capture, he was not arrested until the evening of April 23, when he voluntarily submitted to imprisonment, after having appealed for support through the columns of his leaflet to the Society of the Jacobins and to his followers in general. He was visited in his specially designated room at the Conciergerie, by a large number of solicitous officials, who took care that he received every attention. There was a preliminary hearing of the case on April 23, 1793, which was a sort of rehearsal for the actual performance that was to take place on the next day. Marat denied all the charges, made a high-sounding declaration of his sincerity, declined the proffer of legal assistance, and was recommitted to the *maison de justice*.

When Marat entered the court-room on April 24, he had in his wake a host of supporters gathered from friendly societies and Sections all over the city. He turned to say a few words to the galleries and was applauded. The personnel of the Revolutionary Tribunal was still the same as originally selected on March 13, 1793. The president, Montané, and the public prosecutor, Fouquier-Tinville, who as yet had given no indication of the unhappy vigor that was to characterize his stern measures during the Reign of Terror, had been chosen at a time when the Gironde controlled a majority in the Convention. Brissot in the *Patriote français* had already expressed his confidence in the men who composed this tribunal. Nevertheless, whether because Marat was the first deputy of the people to be hailed before the Revolutionary Tribunal or because they were intimidated by the spectators, who made no secret of their sympathies, it seemed that the entire court was partial to Marat. Twice during the trial Marat felt called upon to urge the spectators not to applaud. The public prosecutor himself appeared anxious to please and succeeded to such an extent that even Marat, who was not easily gratified, approved of his "zeal and resolution." After a slight commotion in the gallery and the introduction of some evidence that was not to the point (disproving that a certain young Englishman in Paris had attempted suicide because Marat had murdered Liberty, as the *Patriote français* had alleged), the actual trial was begun. Each charge was put to the defendant separately. His reply to the accusation that he had incited murder and pillage was that he had merely wished to explain a means of avoiding famine (it was his issue of February 25, 1793, which the Girondins pretended to believe was the cause of the food riots of that day, which was under discussion); it had not been his intention to urge France to employ the strenuous efforts that he had described as those of other countries in times of famine. The accusation that he had preached the dictatorship we have already seen him deny flatly. As to vilifying the National Convention and urging its dissolution, that, he claimed, was not in his power; the Convention was the moulder of its own reputation; he had merely urged it to do its duty; the opinion the people had of it depended upon itself and not upon him. There was no more evidence taken, but Marat was allowed to make a plea on his own behalf. He summed up his defense in a long address intended to prove that he was the victim of a Girondin conspiracy. When he sat down, there was a burst of enthusiastic applause. With this the case went to the jury, which deliberated only forty-five minutes. The chairman rendered its unanimous decision in words that leave no doubts as to its partiality:

> I have examined with care the passages cited from the journals of Marat. To appreciate them better, I have not lost sight of the well-known character of the accused and the time in which he wrote. I can not impute criminal and counter-revolutionary intentions to the intrepid defender of the rights of the people. It is difficult to contain one's just indignation when one sees one's country betrayed on all sides; and I declare that I have found nothing in the writings of Marat that seems to me to confirm the crimes of which he is accused.

During the trial all France had been interested in the outcome. Not only did a large audience attend to cheer Marat, but from all over the Republic addresses exhorting Paris to protect him came to the various Sections and patriotic organizations of the city. When, therefore, Marat was thus acquitted by the Revolutionary Tribunal, great acclamations arose throughout the entire room. Civic crowns and wreaths were thrust upon him, and he was carried triumphantly upon the shoulders of a throng of admirers all the way from the court-room to the Convention amid cheering spectators. At the Convention they received permission to enter, which they did, parading along the aisles and shouting for Marat and the Mountain. Thus did the attempt to overwhelm the Mountain lead only to the "triumph of Marat." On that day there was also a demonstration of rejoicing at the Jacobin Club, and on April 26, when Marat attended the fête given there in his honor, so great was the crowd that one of the stands is reported to have collapsed. There was now no disputing his popular-

ity in the vicinity of Paris.   On May 5, for example, after the
passage of the first law of the maximum, fixing the price of
necessities in France, of which Marat was unjustifiably considered an advocate, cries of *"Marat à la guillotine!"* were
heard, but they were isolated and random and nothing came
of them.   Not so very long before Marat would have had to
take to his cellars once such a cry was raised.

It was now but a question of time until the Girondins
should feel the power of the man they had tried to destroy.
They were to find that in establishing a precedent by sending
Marat before the Revolutionary Tribunal, they had thrown a
boomerang that would return to their own destruction.   On
April 8, 1793, even before the impeachment of Marat, the
Section de Bonconseil sent a deputation to the Convention to
denounce several Girondins by name.   Another declaration
of like nature from thirty-five out of the forty-eight Sections
of Paris was presented by Pache, the mayor of the city, on
April 15, after Marat had been voted "of accusation."   The
"triumph of Marat" shortly afterwards showed that the Paris
populace trusted and loved the Mountain as much as it feared
and hated the Girondins.   The latter, nevertheless, continued
to control a sufficient number of the votes of the Plain to be
able to elect their partisans to the presidency of the Convention.   On May 16 they put their comrade Isnard into the
chair.   Soon afterwards, feeling the danger of remaining
longer in Paris, they began, as Marat had predicted they
would, to agitate for the removal of the Convention from the
Tuileries, where it was then sitting, to the city of Bourges.
Barère, the spokesman of the Committee of Public Safety and
a leader of the Plain, induced them to accept a compromise—
to consent to the establishment of a Commission of Twelve
which should investigate the disturbances in Paris and examine the illegal acts of the Paris Commune and the self-
constituted insurrectionary committees.   This commission,

composed largely of Girondins and their supporters, proceeded immediately to make matters worse by imprisoning the popular Hébert, a leader of the Municipality, who had been a partisan of Marat in his scurrilous sheet *Le Père Duchesne*, and Dobsen, the president of the Section de Cité. On May 25, a petition demanding the suppression of the Committee of Twelve was brought before the Convention. Isnard's reply to the petitioners was his famous-infamous threat that if anything should happen to the national representatives, "Paris would be destroyed, and it would be necessary to inquire upon the banks of the Seine whether Paris had ever existed." His language recalled the Brunswick manifesto—that if anything were to happen to Louis XVI, Paris would pay the penalty The reaction in both cases was similar—a popular uprising.

As was natural, Marat was to be found in the vanguard of the persecutors of the Girondins. On May 27, he moved that the Commission of Twelve be suppressed, arguing that the fear of a plot on the part of the people of Paris was imaginary, a malicious invention of the Girondins to discredit the capital. A long discussion ensued, during which the cry went up that the Convention was surrounded by armed men. Marat, who now carried weapons with him constantly, advanced, pistol in hand, to make inquiries, and found that the men were an armed guard that had been sent to protect the Convention. The Commandant of this detachment later created a stir in the Convention when he protested to the president that Marat had ordered his arrest. Marat declared that the man lied; and during the disturbance that followed the president felt obliged to call the attention of the Convention to the menacing attitude that Marat was taking toward him personally. But the debate went on and toward the end of the session, the Commission of Twelve was abolished and its acts annulled. Two hundred deputies, however, protested that the lateness of the hour, the absence of a number of their colleagues, and the disorders that had attended the voting all rendered the decision illegal. On the next day the motion was reconsidered and now a sufficient effort was put forth by the Girondins to reëstablish the Twelve. In the meantime several of the Sections of Paris and the patriotic clubs had declared themselves *en permanence* and had drawn up plans for insurrection. On May 30 another petition was submitted by a majority of the Sections, demanding the expulsion and arrest of the Commission of Twelve and their supporters. It received no attention. That evening Marat addressed the central revolutionary committee that had established itself at the Évêché, and urged them to arm for a final conflict with the Girondins.[1] On the next day (May 31) the meeting of the Convention opened to the ringing of the tocsin and the boom of the *générale*, both on several previous occasions the heralds of insurrection. This had sufficient weight with a large enough number of the Plain to induce them to vote with the Mountain and again the Commission of Twelve was suppressed.

On June 1 the Convention was still engaged in bitter controversy. While the debates were in progress, Marat left the hall in order to visit the home of a patriot who had evidence to give against some suspected aristocrats. On his way back, he claimed, he was surrounded by large crowds who cried to him, "Marat, save us!" He left the Convention again shortly and went, first, to the Committee of General Security and, then, to the Committee of Public Safety, where he urged the necessity of another meeting of the Convention that evening to bring about the arrest of the Commission of Twelve together with the twenty-two Girondins designated in the petition of the Sections. On the request of the Committee of Public Safety he went with Mayor Pache to the General Council of

---

[1] Esquiros, *Histoire des Montagnards*, II, p. 350. Esquiros claims to have been permitted to use Marat's own notes by Marat's sister Albertine.

the Municipality to avert any premature action, and there re-
minded the insurgents that to rise in revolt was the duty of
the people when their representatives had jeopardized the
safety of the Republic. Having exhorted them to remain under arms until they had obtained their demands regarding the
Girondins, he departed amidst the fervent applause of the
Council. He then returned to the Committee of Public
Safety to render a report of what he had done.

A session of the Convention was held late that evening,
called together by the ringing of the tocsin and the booming
of the *générale*. Only about a hundred representatives were
present and Basire, a Girondin, desired to have the meeting
regarded as invalid because of the paucity of the attendance.
Here another petition against the Girondins was delivered.
Fearing to be accused of having drawn it up, Marat took no
part in the discussion until the very end and only after such
an accusation had actually been made. He spoke briefly in
favor of having the names of Dusaulx, Lanthenas, and Ducos
omitted from the list of the Girondins against whom the petitioners desired action, arguing that these three men were weak
rather than vicious. It was decided to refer the petition to
the Committee of Public Safety for consideration, a report to
be made upon it within three days. Late that night the tocsin
rang and ever since it has been believed, although there is no
adequate ground for the belief, that it was Marat himself
who rang it. More likely it was two members of the revolutionary committee at the Évêché named Varlet and Guzman.

Sunday June 2 started quietly. Marat spent the early part
of the day at the Jacobin Club and again objected to the presence of the names of Dusaulx, Lanthenas, and Ducos upon the
petition. After his arrival at the Convention, the Committee
of Public Safety through Barère made its report, again attempting to compromise with the suggestion that the implicated deputies be allowed to resign. In replying to this

Marat argued that to allow representatives under the displeasure of the people to resign would be to give them an opportunity to pose as martyrs for the cause of public peace. He reserved the right of resignation for genuine patriots such as himself and expressed his willingness to tender his own resignation after the Convention had been made safe for the Republic. Further discussion was closed by the announcement that the assembly was surrounded by armed men. Investigation revealed that it was only a group of women crowding the exits that had created this uneasiness. The debate was resumed, but again the cry that the Convention was surrounded was raised, and this time it was discovered that Henriot's National Guard, equipped with cannon, was drawn up around the Tuileries, guns trained upon the representatives of the people. In the subsequent confusion it was suggested that the Convention make its way from the hall under the leadership of Hérault de Séchelles, who was then acting in the place of the chairman. This was done, though Marat and a handful of Montagnards remained scornfully behind. As the deputies went out, they were greeted with cheers of *"Vive Marat! Vive la Montagne!"* Inside the galleries began to murmur. Marat, to satisfy them, went after the retreating deputies, who by this time had been refused exit by Henriot and were looking aimlessly for some means of egress, and induced (Harmand de la Meuse says "ordered") them to return.

The discussion was resumed. The memoirs of several persons who witnessed these events and contemporary opinion in general concur in granting to Marat the predominant voice in the decisions that followed. His suggestion to exclude from the proscription the names of Dusaulx, Lanthenas, and Ducos was accepted without debate; and in their places were added, also by his motions, the names of Louvet, Valazé, Clavière, and Lebrun. Finally, a decree of arrest was passed against thirty-one of the Girondins, including their greatest leaders—

Vergniaud, Brissot, Pétion, Guadet, Barbaroux, Buzot, and Rabaut-Saint Étienne. Some of them made good their escape, but twenty-two were eventually to meet death upon the guillotine on October 30, 1793, after a hasty trial by the Revolutionary Tribunal.

With the fall of the Girondins, Marat felt that his work in the Convention was done. Seriously ill since the preceding December, he had announced his intention of resigning as soon as the Girondins were overthrown. True to his promise, he offered his resignation to the Convention the day after he had made his announcement to that effect (June 3). The Convention took no action on it, however. In fact, over a month after he had tendered it, he was appointed a member of the Committee on Colonial Affairs. Marat's disease, which hitherto seemed to have been nothing more than acute pruritus, contracted in 1788 and aggravated by his having lived in underground places of hiding, was now complicated by some lung complaint. It had become so serious that he was obliged to seek relief from the severe pain and irritation it caused him by remaining immersed in a bath-tub. The curious may still see in the Musée Grévin in Paris, playing a prominent part in the reproduction of the scene of Marat's assassination, what the owners claim to be the original of his bathtub. It is built like a shoe, in such a way that he could do his work and entertain his visitors almost with propriety. But his working days were fast coming to an end. His journal now consisted almost entirely of letters from correspondents. His own interest was largely monopolized by the ineffectiveness of the Revolutionary Committee of Public Safety to which he now devoted all the attention he had formerly spent upon the dictatorship. Perhaps he foresaw that eventually it would assume dictatorial powers and act as he had wanted his dictator to act. But for the present he was dissatisfied with it. He had confidence in very few of its members and believed that its powers were too restricted.   Since the Convention had not accepted his resignation and was not giving his letters the attention that he thought they deserved, on June 17 he tried to resume his duties as deputy.   But two days of the old strain proved to be all that he could endure and he was again forced back to his home and his tub.

His last days were filled with apprehension because remnants of the Capetian house still survived and the wave of internal disorder continued to rise steadily.   Lyons, Grenoble, Marseilles, and the Vendée were in open revolt.   Several of the Girondins who had escaped were fomenting rebellion in Normandy.   He offered to lead an army against the rebels himself, if his health would permit.   "I am not a stranger to the military art," he boasted, "and I could without vaunting answer for my success."   This civil war was to be the direct cause of his death.   It was from Normandy that a young lady, a descendant of the poet Corneille, came to assassinate the Friend of the People.   Marie-Anne-Charlotte Corday d'Armans was a romantic soul of conservative instincts, whose favorite reading was Plutarch and the Biblical account of Judith.   She had been shocked by the maltreatment of the Girondins, some of whom, including Barbaroux, she had met in her native town of Caen after their expulsion from the Convention.   Anxious to become a martyr in the cause of liberty, she went secretly to Paris to kill the leaders of the Jacobins, particularly Marat, whom she regarded as the author of all of her country's ills.   She took with her a letter of introduction from Barbaroux to the Deputy Duperret, through whom she hoped to gain access to the Tuileries, there amidst the most appropriate and stately of settings to immolate her victim.   Failing to find Marat at the Convention, however, she sought him at his home.   Her first request to be admitted into the loathsome presence was refused by Simonne Evrard.   The Friend of the People, she was told, was too ill to receive visitors. She returned to the room that she had rented and wrote Marat a letter:

> I come from Caen. Your love for the country ought to make you anxious to know the plots that are being laid there. I await your reply.

A curious letter, indeed, to be addressed to one who is soon to be punished by the writer for his selfishness toward his country. But perhaps she felt that to appeal to the hypocrite it was necessary to humor his hypocrisy. Her note was delivered to Marat in the evening of July 13. Without waiting for his answer, however, Charlotte Corday presented herself at his door about eight o'clock. She was about to be sent away for a second time, when Marat, who had heard her voice raised in protest, called that she be permitted to enter. What followed we learn from Charlotte's own testimony at her trial.

"What is going on at Caen?" he asked her after she had taken her seat.

"Eighteen deputies from the Convention rule there in collusion with the Department."

"What are their names?"

She gave them as Marat wrote them down.

"They will soon be guillotined," he said.[1]

With that Charlotte Corday arose and plunged a knife into his lungs. He was able only to cry for help before he died. Simonne Evrard rushed in first, followed by a flock of neighbors. After a brief struggle Charlotte Corday was made a prisoner. Marat was taken from his bath for medical attention that was of no avail. A cross-examination of the assassin by police officials revealed the motives of her act: "having seen civil war on the verge of blazing out all over France and

---

[1] Such, at least, was her first testimony. Later she changed this last statement of Marat's to "I will soon have them guillotined." Although the change is of no importance, the first statement seems the more likely.

persuaded that Marat was the principal author of this disaster, I preferred to make the sacrifice of my life in order to save my country." A search of her person revealed the sheath of the knife and a second letter that she had intended to use if her second attempt to see Marat failed:

> I wrote you this morning, Marat. Have you received my letter? I can not believe it, since I have been turned from your door. I hope that to-morrow you will grant me an interview. I repeat to you, I come from Caen. I have secrets to reveal to you that are most important for the welfare of the Republic. Furthermore, I am persecuted in the cause of liberty. I am unhappy. That is sufficient to give me the right to your protection.

As she was taken to jail only the greatest efforts of her custodians saved her from being torn to pieces by the infuriated mob. She sank exhausted into her carriage, surprised that she was still alive. Since she made practically no defense, her trial was soon over and she was guillotined on July 17. At Caen her Bible was said to have been found open at the story of Judith.

It was on July 14, 1793, the fourth anniversary of the Fall of the Bastille, that the last number of Marat's journal appeared. He had been at work upon it shortly before his death. The finishing touch of Marat's editorial pen was typical of the man. It was an attack upon the Committee of Public Safety, particularly its *rapporteur* Barère, for his "floating between two waters" and "paralyzing every vigorous measure" of the Committee. Thus ended the career of Jean Paul Marat. He had but recently turned fifty years of age, the oldest of the prominent figures of the Revolution, with the exception of Necker, Bailly, Malouet, and Roland. For revolutions are the work of young men.

The state of Marat's finances at the time of his death may be surmised from the fact that an inventory of his possessions, made by the municipal authorities after his assassination, showed that his entire money-wealth consisted of an assignat for twenty-five sous. Among the manuscripts that he left, in addition to those already mentioned, were a *Mémoire sur les Expériences que Newton donne en preuve du système de la différente refrangibilité des rayons hétérogènes*, an *Analyse de différents systèmes sur le feu, la chaleur, congélation et thermomètre*, a discussion of the *Cristal d'Islande et du Brasil*, a *Discours sur le moyen de perfectionner l'Encyclopédie*, some notes on the *Administration des finances*, and a few pages entitled *Histoire de la Révolution*. The manuscripts of a scientific nature were probably works that he had laid aside at the outbreak of the Revolution, intending to complete them for publication at some future date. The one on the *Cristal d'Islande*, for example, he had already mentioned in his *Mémoires Académiques* of 1788. The fragmentary state of his papers on finance and the history of the Revolution bear eloquent witness to his lack of leisure during the Revolution and to the fact that his contribution to the development of the Revolution had been practical rather than theoretical, as a maker rather than as a writer of history.

CHAPTER VI

D ISRAELI, commenting upon the death of Abraham Lincoln, once said:

Assassination has never changed the history of the world. I will not refer to the remote past, although an accident has made the most memorable example of antiquity at this moment fresh in the mind and memory of all present. But even the costly sacrifice of a Cæsar did not propitiate the inexorable destiny of his country. If we look to modern times, to times at least with the feelings of which we are familiar, and the people of which are animated and influenced by the same interest as ourselves, the violent deaths of two heroic men, Henry IV of France and the Prince of Orange, are conspicuous illustrations of this truth.

At first glance it would appear that the assassination of Marat was another conspicuous illustration of this truth. The Marat whose murder forms the only title to fame of Charlotte Corday was but a shadowy wisp of his former self. Wretchedly ill and despairing of recovery, he had begun to limit his energies to the edition of his journal, which now contained comparatively few of his own words, and to occasional letters to the Convention, which were regularly disregarded. It is highly probable that, in any case, he could not have lived very much longer. He himself—and he seems to have acted as his own physician—spoke of his health in despondent tones. But even if he had managed to drag out his painful and miserable existence for several more years, his influence would have waned as his activities became less and less conspicuous and his writings lost their trenchancy and vigor.

In the case of a great many figures of historical importance the same statement can be made with equal truth—that they outlived their usefulness and, accordingly, their influence. But it would have been peculiarly true of Marat, had not Charlotte Corday's knife found its goal at the supreme moment. In order to understand why this was so, we must answer several questions. What was his influence? How did it develop? Upon what did it depend? To answer these inquiries it will be necessary to review his entire career and to repeat points that have already been made. But the answers are important: the significance of any historical character depends not so much upon what he did, said, or thought as upon the influence that his deeds, words, and opinions had upon the events and the people of his own and subsequent eras.

We may start with the generalization, fallible though generalizations are, that at no time was Marat's influence due to his political ideas. Before the Revolution whatever popularity he enjoyed was attributable to his reputation as a physician and scientist. To be sure, he had written several works of a political nature, but they had been incidental and had not contributed greatly toward his fame. His writings of the early revolutionary period were of a moderate character, similar to a myriad of other works and possessing no distinguishing features. If, as he claimed, his *Offrande à la patrie*, published on the dawn of the Revolution, was crowned by a patriotic society, that is an indication less of its intrinsic merit or influence than of the fact that such societies were very numerous and not over-discriminating in approving brochures of a patriotic spirit. It was not until the establishment of his daily journal that Marat became a figure of importance in the French Revolution. This is shown by the sudden increase in the amount of attention devoted to him by the Paris Commune and the National Assembly, the nu-

merous attempts to arrest him, and the counter measures of the
Cordeliers to protect him. But it was not his political philosophy that caused this alignment for and against him; it
was his attacks upon Necker, Lafayette, Bailly, and other
alleged counter-revolutionaries. It was his destructive invective and not any constructive ideology that won him both
his enemies and his friends.

Yet, by this time he was beginning to set forth a definite
political program. He advocated the formation of revolutionary clubs, but prematurely—when a few pioneers, such
as the Breton Club, already existed, but before they were
ready to become an active part of the political machinery of
the Revolution. The clubs that eventually were formed developed gradually, largely as a matter of political exigency,
and were not the product of any deliberate attempts at arti-
ficial cultivation such as Marat had advocated. By the time
the clubs had begun to be a factor in politics, Marat had already gone on to another demand—the revolutionary tribunal.
Again he was ahead of the times. The idea of a judicial body
created for the express purpose of punishing political offenders did not seize the popular imagination for three more years.
And in the meantime Marat had begun to support still another
project—the dictatorship. This, however, was the least popular of all his political schemes. Marat himself admitted
that he had been unable to obtain any support in preaching
it and that he was entirely alone among all the thinkers of
the Revolution in championing it. And yet it is his chief
contribution to revolutionary philosophy—the theory which
he advocated longest and most consistently. Admission of
its unpopularity was tantamount to admission of the unpopularity of his whole scheme of political philosophy. Of his
constructive policies, therefore, there remains only his support
of the revolutionary committees, such as the Committee of
Public Safety, which was the only plan that he advocated

opportunely and successfully. This idea, however, was not his; he was but one of many to champion it and, as has been shown, there is good reason to believe that he recommended it only because it came nearest to a realization of his dictatorship program, which had become too obnoxious to the people at large for him to continue openly as its exponent.

These are the several phases of Marat's constructive politics. They entitle him, to be sure, to generous credit for his political insight, but the fact nevertheless remains that they did not appeal to the minds of his dearly-beloved people. It was his attacks and not his proposals that won their support. It was because he constantly feared counter-revolution and threw himself bodily upon it wherever he beheld it that he became known as a whole-hearted supporter of the Revolution. He made prediction upon prediction of disastrous conspiracies that were afoot to overthrow the achievements of recent years, for prediction was a form of accusation. He claimed that three hundred of these vaticinations came true, and if here again his curious conception of numbers plays him false, it can nevertheless not be denied that a few of these prophecies were astonishingly correct. For example, Mirabeau was actually in the employ of the court; the King did attempt to take flight; Lafayette did desert; Dumouriez did prove to be a traitor. With each such successful prediction his reputation as a guardian of the Revolution increased. Camille Desmoulins called him *Cassandra Marat*, for his prophetic vision, though god-given, remained unheeded by man. Marat's prognostications, of course, were thus a double-edged weapon, effective both in defense and offense. The more he attacked his enemies, the more predictions he made; the more predictions he made, the more came true; the more came true, the greater grew his reputation and popularity.

But it was not by attacks and predictions alone that Marat

showed himself the devotee of the Revolution. He had
suffered for it more than any other. Everybody knew (Marat
took care that they should learn) of the seven or more attempts to arrest him, of his frequent hiding in unwholesome
places, of the seriousness of the resultant illness, of his having lost all his wealth in the service of the people and their
Revolution. He announced, perhaps with some truth, that
he had lived for a period of nine months on only bread and
water in order to furnish the expenses of printing his pamphlets and papers; that "for more than three years [this was
in 1793] he had not taken a quarter of an hour of recreation"
so that he might give more time to his country's needs; that
he "watched day and night" over the safety of the people.
But whether true or not, these statements, repeated with literally hundreds of others of a similar tenor to readers who
were probably as gullible as newspaper-readers have ever
been, had a telling effect. Their admiration and confidence
grew: if he had devoted his life to them, they would be no
less willing to devote their lives to him.

When once he had deserted his bourgeois notions, Marat
deliberately cultivated the favor of the lower classes. The
phrase *Ami du Peuple*, which he now used not only to describe
his journal but also as a title that accompanied his signature
even on official papers, had been chosen advisedly. But his
program of labor and social reform, though derived from a
sincere conviction of the injustice of the economic organization
of society and probably emphasized in order to win for him
the support of the populace, was no more heeded than his
political program. More profitable than this was his deliberate imitation of the dress of the lower classes. Contemporary portraits and memoirs bear witness to his unkempt
clothes and uncouth manner. He who had once had a marquise for a mistress was now a *sans-culotte*, wore his shirt
open at the neck, a bandage around his head, and pistols in

his belt. Fabre d'Eglantine has left us a detailed description of him. Marat, he says,

> was short of stature, scarcely five feet high. He was nevertheless of a firm, thick-set figure, without being stout. His shoulders and chest were broad, the lower part of his body thin, thigh short and thick, legs bowed, and strong arms, which he employed with great vigor and grace. Upon a rather short neck he carried a head of a very pronounced character. He had a large and bony face, aquiline nose, flat and slightly depressed, the under part of the nose prominent; the mouth medium-sized and curled at one corner by a frequent contraction; the lips were thin, the forehead large, the eyes of a yellowish grey color, spirited, animated, piercing, clear, naturally soft and ever gracious and with a confident look; the eyebrows thin, the complexion thick and skin withered, chin unshaven, hair brown and neglected. He was accustomed to walk with head erect, straight and thrown back, with a measured stride that kept time with the movement of his hips. His ordinary carriage was with his two arms firmly crossed upon his chest. In speaking in society he always appeared much agitated, and almost invariably ended the expression of a sentiment by a movement of the foot, which he thrust rapidly forward, stamping it at the same time on the ground, and then rising on tiptoe, as though to lift his short stature to the height of his opinion. The tone of his voice was thin, sonorous, slightly hoarse, and of a ringing quality. A defect of the tongue rendered it difficult for him to pronounce clearly the letters *c* and *l*, to which he was accustomed to give the sound *g*. There was no other perceptible peculiarity except a rather heavy manner of utterance; but the beauty of his thought, the fullness of his eloquence, the simplicity of his elocution, and the point of his speeches absolutely effaced the maxillary heaviness. At the tribune, if he rose without obstacle or excitement, he stood with assurance and dignity, his right hand upon his hip, his left arm extended upon the desk in front of him, his head thrown back, turned toward his audience at three-quarters, and a little inclined toward his right shoulder. If on the contrary he had to vanquish at the tribune the shrieking of chicanery and bad faith or the despotism of the president, he awaited the reëstablishment of order in silence and resuming his speech with firmness, he adopted a bold attitude, his arms crossed diagonally upon his chest, his figure bent for-

ward toward the left.   His face and his look at such times acquired an almost sardonic character, which was not belied by the
cynicism of his speech.   He dressed in a careless manner; indeed,
his negligence in this respect announced a complete neglect of the
conventions of custom and of taste and, one might almost say,
gave him an air of uncleanliness.

Barras tells us that when he first saw Napoleon Bonaparte he
was struck forcibly by the resemblance to Marat.   What an
impression this queer little Friend of the People must have
made upon the popular imagination as he walked along the
streets of Paris, or, with his grim smile, delivered his sometimes eloquent and always defiant addresses from the tribune!
How strange he must have seemed to the guests of the actor
Thalma on that autumn night of 1792, when he broke in,
unbidden, with pistols, bandage, and shirt *à la* Lord Byron,
upon the party given in honor of the great Dumouriez!
What the attitude of the people toward Marat must have
been, Camille Desmoulins summed up in a pat manner, once
when Marat had been attacked at the Convention with more
than usual vehemence:

> Say what you will, Marat against whom you demand a decree
> of accusation, is perhaps the only man who can save the Republic.
> . . . Fortunately we have Marat, who by his subterranean life
> and his indefatigable labors is regarded as the acme of patriotism
> and holds that position so well established that it will always ap-
> pear to the people that beyond what Marat proposes there can be
> only delirium and extravagance. . . . This is the great service
> that he alone is in a position to render to the Republic: he will
> always prevent the counter-revolution from masking itself in red
> cockades.

Panis, too, on a former occasion had likewise reflected this
popular opinion:

> Marat is an extraordinary man outside of the common run.   He
> does not sleep.   He is ceaselessly occupied with the public welfare.
> His experience, his extensive knowledge have enabled him to predict
> everything that has happened.   With his ardent spirit and lively

imagination, always bent upon the same object, is it astonishing that he says extraordinary things?

Marat himself realized very well why he was popular. In his first interview with Robespierre, when the Incorruptible protested against his virulent addresses, Marat replied:

> Learn that my reputation with the people rests, not upon my ideas, but upon my boldness, upon the impetuous outbursts of my soul, upon my cries of rage, of despair, and of fury against the rascals who impede the action of the Revolution. I am the anger, the just anger, of the people and that is why they listen to me and believe in me. These cries of alarm and of fury that you take for empty words are the most naïve and most sincere expressions of the passions that devour my soul.

Such, indeed, were the reasons for the esteem in which Marat was held, an esteem which in part was cultivated and in part was the natural result of his political sympathies. It was not due to his ideas or to his program, but to his character, his language, his attacks, his apparent sincerity and devotion to the cause of the Revolution.

It must not be thought, however, that he had always been a popular idol. At the very beginning of the Revolution, whatever fame he enjoyed was entirely local. The local office of elector in the Assembly of his District was the only one with which he was honored until September 1792. For over three years, at a time when public employment was comparatively easy to secure, Marat held no government post. His letters to members of the National Assembly were not even given the courtesy of an answer. His presentation of one of his works to that body passed without comment. On the other hand, several districts of the city protested in one way or another against his caustic attacks. But during those three years his influence matured. To prove this, one need only point to the intense desire of his enemies to silence him.

There were at least seven attempts to arrest him and to suppress his paper during 1789 and 1790. The Commune devoted a large part of its time to discussing his activities.
Even the national representative bodies—first the National Assembly and then the Legislative Assembly—were called upon,
on at least four different occasions, to consider measures aimed
directly at his journal. On the other hand, the amount of
support that he received from various sources points likewise
to his growing power. Danton and the Cordeliers took him
under their special protection in December 1789 and almost
engaged in street fighting in order to defend him from arrest.
Other journalists—Desmoulins, Loustalot, Prudhomme—at
various times spoke favorably of him. Fréron, the editor of
the *Orateur du Peuple*, soon to become the leader of the icon-
oclasts of the Thermidorian Reaction, at this time put his
paper at the disposal of Marat and permitted him to edit
several of his numbers. The *Vainqueurs de la Bastille* in a
letter to the National Assembly included him upon a list of
the journalists who had best served the cause of liberty
(August 1, 1790). A letter dated October 8, 1790 testifies
that the writer had witnessed a crowd listening to the reading
of lengthy passages from the *Ami du Peuple* attacking the
King's ministers. And already in 1791 (as again in 1793)
the youthful St. Just had been roused to the point of eulogy
in admiration of him.

Finally there is indubitable testimony of his increasing
popularity in the fact that many forgeries of his journal,
parading under the same name or ones similar to it, began to
appear. During Marat's first sojourn in England in 1790
there were several unauthentic continuations of the *Ami du
Peuple;* and upon resumption of the journal in 1792, after
his second stay in England, he found it desirable to prefix to
the first few numbers a letter from the Society of the Cordeliers urging him to continue the paper, in order to distinguish

the true issues from the spurious ones that had sprung up in his absence.   These were not the only false editions of the *Ami du Peuple*.   Chevremont, a recent bibliographer of Marat's works, considered it necessary to devote about half of a large volume on the writings of Marat to an analysis of the false and the true issues of his various journals.   There were also several papers which devoted large amounts of their space to refuting and counteracting his theories.   The chief of these was one with the title of *L'Anti-Marat*.   Since one does not attack or support or imitate a totally obscure person, it may be deduced that Marat had won a reputation of some magnitude during 1790, 1791, and the early part of 1792. But he was not yet a leader with any great personal following. We have seen that when he was suggested as a candidate for the Legislative Assembly, he received only two votes out of a possible seven hundred and thirty-nine.   On May 3, 1792, when the Legislative Assembly passed a decree of outlawry against him, not a single voice was to be found to speak in his defense.   Chevremont and Bougeart, the two biographers who are most biased in Marat's favor, concur in the belief that he could not have found at this time more than two hundred supporters throughout the breadth of France.

But Marat's hour of triumph was not far off.   On August 10, 1792, the revolutionary force overwhelmed the royalists. In Paris this was a distinct lower-class victory—of the proletariat over the bourgeoisie, of the populace led by Robespierre and Marat over the middle classes led by Lafayette and Pétion.   Thereafter in revolutionary astrology there was no star more auspicious than Marat's.   Honors poured in upon him.   He was granted the royal presses for his own use.   The Commune appointed him its official reporter, although there is no reason to believe he actually functioned in this capacity. He was chosen a member of the electoral assembly of his Section and later of the electoral assembly of Paris.   He was appointed a member of the Committee of Police and Surveillance of the Commune. And finally he was elected by an overwhelming majority a member of the National Convention, the seventh of the twenty-four of the Paris delegation, preceded only by persons of well-recognized popularity. Furthermore, none of the candidates whom he had opposed in his editorial articles was chosen to represent Paris.[1]

Thereafter Marat identified himself with the Mountain and his vogue rose and fell with that of his party. Marat himself had constantly claimed to belong to no party, to recognize no ties save those dictated by his loyalty to the people. But in the Convention he sat with the Mountain, shared their loves and hates, attacked and was attacked with them. Several of the Girondins professed to see in him, rather than in Danton or Robespierre, the leader of the Left. Buzot was convinced that at the Jacobins "Marat was chief; Danton and Robespierre commanded only as subalterns." Meillan assures us that "he had at his beck that class of people who can neither see nor judge and who are always for the man who cajoles them," and that "such support made him redoubtable despite the contempt with which he was covered." And Louvet de Couvrai believed that among the Cordeliers "the apparent chiefs were Danton and Robespierre; the secret chief, Marat." At any rate, the denunciations of the Girondins fell most heavily upon him.

The members of the Mountain, however, were not altogether enthusiastic adherents of Marat. Danton, although one of Marat's earliest supporters, had quarreled with him amidst the anguish of the September Massacres over the arrest of Adrien Duport and twice thereafter (September 25 and October 29, 1792) spoke of him in disparaging tones before

---

[1] Kropotkin, *Great French Revolution*, p. 309, says that only those whom Marat had endorsed were elected. This, however, is incorrect, as a comparison of Marat's placards with the roll of the Paris delegation will show. There were some elected of whom Marat had said not a word.

the Convention. "I declare to the Convention," he said on
one of these occasions, "and to the entire nation that I do
not like the individual Marat. (*Applause.*) I say frankly
that I have had experience with his temper. He is not only
volcanic and bitter but unsociable." Both Robespierre, who
had advocated Marat's election to the Convention, and Panis,
whose candidacy for the mayoralty Marat had favored in
September 1792 and who had appointed him to the Committee
of Police and Surveillance, repudiated him on September 25,
1792, when the first and one of the most bitter onslaughts of
the Girondins was directed against him, and he had had to
face a hostile house alone. Desmoulins, who was generally
lavish in his admiration of Marat, nevertheless had been
spoken of with frank contempt in the *Ami du Peuple* and had
replied in kind. Robert, who never doubted Marat's patriotism (for that matter, very few ever questioned Marat's sincere
patriotism) and yet felt that he was extravagant in his pas-
sions, once, in denouncing this extravagance, unintentionally
started a movement to oust him from the Society of the
Jacobins. And in spite of the facts that the Jacobins had
staunchly forwarded Marat's campaign for election to the
Convention, that he regarded them as his chief protectors
against his enemies, that he was frequently lionized and applauded at their meetings, and that he later became their pre-
siding officer, this movement received a surprising amount of
support, although it resulted in failure; all that the Society
would agree to do was to address a circular to its sister chapters
detailing the distinction that it drew between Robespierre and
Marat "in order that they might learn once and for all to
separate the two names which they wrongfully believe ought
constantly to be united." Some months afterward (May 31,
1793) Robert again renewed the attempt because of Marat's
demand for a dictator, and this time Billaud-Varennes joined
forces with him. But that this attack also failed we have

already learned. Regardless of personal likes and dislikes, the Mountain had to show a united front to the multiplying charges of the Girondins, and Marat's now known and firmly established influence with the lower classes was too great for them to disregard. Camille Desmoulins' retort to the Girondins will be remembered: "Fortunately we have Marat. . . ."

To add to the strength of Marat's position there was the weight of his paper. Since the opening of the Convention he had distributed gratis six or seven hundred copies of it daily. Indeed, on some days very many more than that number were thus issued. These went almost entirely to members of the Mountain and to the popular societies, where, it may be assumed, each copy was read by more than one person. Since Marat had no independent source of income he probably earned the money necessary for this free distribution of his journal from the sale of the remainder of his daily impressions. Therefore the circulation of the *Ami du Peuple* and its various successors was probably much more than six or seven hundred, perhaps two or three times that number. In a day when printing was a slow and tedious process and newspapers were expensive, this was a large subscription list. Hatin, the standard authority on the history of journalism in France, says that Marat exercised the greatest influence of all the journalists of the Revolution, and contemporary opinion agrees with this statement. "One word inserted in his sheet," Meillan said, "sufficed to arouse the populace and could occasion an insurrection." And Beaulieu, speaking of Fréron's *Orateur du Peuple* and Marat's *Ami du Peuple*, gave as his opinion that "it is impossible to calculate the effects that these sheets, disgusting with blood, produced upon the lower classes; the last of these individuals especially, a maniac without ability, a kind of crazy idiot whom one must have seen and heard to have any conception of, became the divinity

of the populace; although he was an instrument in the hands
of more adroit people, he succeeded in making them all trem-
ble without himself doubting his prodigious power."

Marat's influence made itself felt when the Convention
debated whether to hale him before the Revolutionary Tribunal. The vote taken on that occasion was determined entirely by party exigencies. With few exceptions the Mountain voted for Marat with appropriate words of praise and
the Girondins voted against him with equally appropriate
words of condemnation. The result of the trial was merely
to enhance Marat's favor in the eyes of his followers. Had he
not been unjustly persecuted? Had not the struggle that had
earned him all his enemies been carried on for the welfare of
the people? Were not his enemies also the sworn enemies of
the people? The support of the popular societies was a fore-
gone conclusion, since the decree of accusation had been passed
while he was president of the Jacobins. Outside of Paris feeling was just as keen. In Chartres hawkers of newspapers attacking Marat were mobbed; and the commune of Auxerre
wrote to the Jacobins commending his safety to the forty-
eight Sections of Paris.

Then came his acquittal and triumphs in the Convention
on April 24 and at the Jacobins on April 26. The inevitable
consequence of the failure of the Girondins and the triumph
of Marat was their own destruction. There is no need to
repeat here the narrative of the events of May 27 to June 2.
For our immediate purposes it is sufficient to indicate that
Marat was undoubtedly the guiding genius, the uncrowned dictator, of those days. It was he who brought about the first abolition of the Committee of Twelve. It was he who addressed
the Committee of the Évêché and the *Conseil Général*, urging
upon them the duty of insurrection. It was he who prevented the success of Barère's compromise plans. It was he
who induced the bewildered deputies who had left the Tuile-

ries to return to the discussion of the fate of the accused. And finally it was he whose motions determined the names ultimately retained upon the proscription list. In previous revolutionary crises his part had been small. The Fourteenth of July, the Fifth of October, the Tenth of August were the heydays of other popular leaders. Even the Second of September, we have seen, was due only indirectly to him. But the Second of June was Marat's doing, more than Robespierre's, more than Danton's, more than Henriot's.

This was the high tide of Marat's popularity. Even in the short period that still remained of his life, it was evident that his influence was beginning to ebb. His paper was losing its passionate vigor. His letters to the Convention received no attention, now that the Mountain no longer needed his support against the Girondins. Not even his resignation called forth any definite action. Despite his great victory, no honor save the insignificant one of membership in a minor committee was accorded him. The popular societies still sent delegations to inquire after his health and seemed much perturbed that he got no better, but with them, too, his power was bound to wane since he could no longer attend their meetings. Unless some cure of his illness could have been effected, Marat must have become a supernumerary in the revolutionary drama. It was probably at this time that he undertook a revision of the *Ami du Peuple* with the intention of republishing the complete files. If so, it was a silent but eloquent admission that his glory lay in the past. It was a man who was already dying both physically and politically that Charlotte Corday's dagger struck down.

For this reason it would seem true, on a superficial consideration, that Marat's violent death is but another example of Disraeli's contention that assassination never has changed the course of the world's history. But an examination of events after the murder of Marat shows that in a certain sense this generalization is not applicable here. The death of Marat did have a very definite effect upon the course of future developments, although not in a way that Charlotte Corday would have wished. Instead of removing his baneful influence from the world, it made it greater.

The news of the slaying of Marat spread rapidly throughout Paris and the rest of France. The immediate result was to make of him a martyr in the cause of liberty and revolution, a paladin who had given his life for the good of his countrymen. Charlotte Corday personified royalism, Girondism, counter-revolution in every form. There were rumors—not altogether without foundation—that the death of Marat was only the first in a long series of conspiracies against the leaders of the Revolution. Marat, the staunch Friend of the People, was the victim of the bitter enemies of the people. Thus Marat, carried off at a time when ill-health and approaching age would have brought about his oblivion, was made into a national hero, crowned with a martyr's halo.

An elaborate funeral was held at tremendous expense, which the government paid. It was attended by the Convention in a body, by representatives of the Sections of Paris and of the Departments, and by a huge cortège of people. The body lay in state for two days, before early putrefaction made necessary the completion of ceremonies. Memorials took place all over France in his honor. Busts of him were unveiled everywhere with profuse oratory and effervescent sentiments. The Section of the Marseillais changed its name to the Section of Marat. Children and regiments were christened after him. The name Montmartre (the hill, the faubourg, the street) became everywhere Montmarat. The Place de l'Observance became the Place de l'Ami du Peuple. The future Marshal Murat, brother-in-law of the Emperor Napoleon and King of Naples, is said to have changed his name temporarily to Marat. No less than thirty-seven towns are on record as having assumed the name of Marat. The St. Eustache Club, a women's organization, seconded by the Society of the Jacobins, erected a wooden obelisk to his memory. Poems and dramas were written about him or dedicated to him. Hymns were sung and speeches pronounced comparing him to Jesus —at least once to Jesus' disparagement. At the theatre, the club, the wine shop, the street corner, everyone talked of Marat. His heart was embalmed and enshrined at the old church of the Cordeliers, now the seat of the Club of the Cordeliers, like the saintly relics of the Middle Ages. His body found a temporary resting-place in the Club's garden.

A well-defined *culte de Marat* sprang up, and people were expected to wear some memento of him. His name became one to conjure with, and even Danton, denounced at the Jacobins by Robespierre, called upon "the ghost of Marat" for justification. His statue, sculptured by David, adorned the hall where the Convention met. In February 1794, a small group of people, including the famous actress Fleury with whom Marat is sometimes, though on insufficient grounds, supposed to have been closely associated, were released from prison for no other reason than that they claimed to have befriended Marat at a time when he was in peril from the police. In the Paris Commune, someone, supported by Hébert, made the motion (August 14, 1793) that copies of his *Chaînes de l'Esclavage* be distributed among the primary assemblies as an infallible antidote to despotism. A complete edition of his writings was planned and the prospectus published, but the work was halted by Robespierre, who feared that it might weaken his party.

Several spurious continuations of his journal were issued. One of these was for a time conducted under the auspices of the Cordeliers. Another was by Jacques Roux, a leader of the *Enragés*, whose extreme radicalism Marat had so strenuously opposed as to lead to a momentary suspicion that Roux was an accomplice of Charlotte Corday. But now, glorying in the title of *le petit Marat* in addition to that of *Marat of the Conseil Général*, which he had formerly arrogated to himself, Roux published *Le Publiciste de la République française, par l'Ombre de Marat, l'ami du peuple*. Leclerc d'Oze, another of the *Enragés*, published a similar journal under the title of *Ami du Peuple*. There was also an *Ami du Peuple par Cxxx* of which the sixteenth number appeared as late as 21 Nivôse An 3 (January 10, 1795), at a time when feeling against Marat's memory ran at its highest.

Both Jacques Roux and Leclerc d'Oze had been denounced by Marat at the Club of the Cordeliers and in his journal shortly before his death and, as a result of his and Robespierre's opposition, had been expelled from that organization. Within a month after Marat's assassination Simonne Evrard complained (August 8, 1793) to the Convention that by continuing his paper and filling it with their extreme views, they were sullying the reputation of the dead Friend of the People. She admitted that Marat had sometimes had recourse to vigorous language "because his sensitive soul gave vent to just anathemas against public blood suckers and against the oppressors of the people," but Roux and Leclerc, under the protection of Marat's name, were preaching "extravagant maxims that his enemies had imputed to him but all his conduct had disavowed" and thereby perpetuated the "murderous calumny" that he was "an insane apostle of disorder and anarchy." The journals of the two *Enragés* did not long survive this bitter denunciation of *la veuve Marat;* and we may be thankful for the occasion of Simonne Evrard's address, since it permits us to understand how the individual who probably was the closest friend of Marat regarded him.

Marat's widow was right in denying that he was "an insane apostle of disorder and anarchy." But there were many now who had begun to believe that counter-revolution had reached the point where it could be combated only by a stringent policy of terror; and they felt that the memory of Marat was on their side. Such a policy, which had made some feeble beginnings before the assassination of Marat, was accelerated by this latest move of the counter-revolutionists. Within the month immediately following that event, an extraordinary number of repressive measures were passed and carried into effect. To begin with, the fate of the Girondins was sealed. The decree of accusation passed against them on June 2, 1793 had not necessarily meant their death, but now that they were regarded as implicated in the plot against the People's Martyr, their execution became inevitable. Charlotte Corday was tried and executed on July 17. Between July 14 and 28 decrees of accusation were passed against eight deputies who were suspected of having given aid to her and the Girondins. On the motion of Barère, on July 28 eighteen Girondins were outlawed and eleven ordered to be brought before the Revolutionary Tribunal. Between July 30 and August 6 the number of the proscribed rose to fifty-five, because of a series of arrests by order of the revolutionary committees. All of this happened during the month immediately following the death of Marat (although it was not until October 29 that twenty-two of the Girondins were tried and condemned to the guillotine, one committing suicide, the others going to their execution on October 30).

During this same period a series of repressive acts of a general nature were also passed. It was ordained that food monopolists and profiteers were to be punished by death, a step that Marat had always favored in preference to the Maximum. Interference with the functions of patriotic societies became a serious offense. The property of all persons *hors la loi* was to be confiscated. All foreigners who had not had their homes in France before July 14, 1789 were ordered arrested. Frenchmen, under penalty of being outlawed, were prohibited from investing their property abroad. Refusal to accept an assignat or acceptance of one only at a discount was made punishable by twenty years' imprisonment. On August 1 the gates of Paris were closed; and on the next day the theatres were surrounded and several hundreds of young men arrested as aristocrats. All this happened between July 14 and August 14, 1793.

It would be fatuous to claim that this inception of the Reign of Terror was entirely due to the assassination of Marat. To do so would be to lose sight of the various other factors that caused the era of panic of 1793–1794, such as the victories of the Coalition against France, the dissension in the National Convention, the radicalism of the Sections and the Commune, the civil wars in the Departments. But Marat's murder was one of the important contributing causes; it embittered the feelings of the Mountain and of the people of Paris, lent impetus to a movement that would otherwise have come more slowly, and made that movement more savage while the memory of his death remained fresh. It is not without significance, for example, that one of the "infernal columns" of Carrier, perhaps the most thorough agent of the Reign of Terror, called itself *la compagnie Marat*, that the individual troopers in it soon were called Marats, or that the Jacobin prince, Charles of Hesse, who was very active in the work of suppression in Southern France gloried in the "honorable title of General Marat."

The first breach in the Reign of Terror came with the overthrow of Robespierre on July 27, 1794, when the Thermidorian Reaction set in. For a time after the Thermidorian insurrection, Marat's popularity remained powerful, for it was with great surprise and reluctance that the leaders in the downfall of the Robespierre party found themselves regarded by the people as the champions of reaction to the Terror and of re-

turn to normal government.   On August 19, Louchet delivered a long speech to the Convention in which he pleaded for
a continuation "of that inflexible severity to which the judi-
cious and profound Marat never ceased to recall us." On
September 21, 1794 (the last date on the new Revolutionary
Calendar) Marat was given the honors of the Pantheon, the
national hall of fame.   This ceremony had been in preparation for a considerable period of time.   As early as November
1793, amidst great enthusiasm, it was voted by the Convention to extend the glory of Pantheonization to the Friend of
the People.   A few days later, a committee, of which the poet
Chénier was the spokesman, submitted a report to the effect
that Mirabeau, the first Revolutionary character to have been
Pantheonized, was unworthy of the distinction that had already been conferred upon him and that he ought to be replaced in the Pantheon by Marat.   Finally on September 19,
1794, a plan for the celebration of the Pantheonization of the
Friend of the People was drawn up.   No Catholic canoniza-
tion could have been more solemn and elaborate.   Even the
smallest details regarding the costumes to be worn, the hymns
to be sung, and the route that the procession was to take were
regulated by national statute.   Since Mirabeau, Marat was
the first of the statesmen of the Revolution so to be honoured.
The body of the former was taken out and buried in a nearby
cemetery as Marat's entered, for it would have been an in-
dignity to the remains of the dead martyr to lie next to the
venal Constituent whom he had frequently denounced.   Perhaps some ironical witness remembered Marat's cry of joy
when he published the news of Mirabeau's death.

But the ill-feeling against Marat followed shortly upon the
fall of the party with which he had been affiliated.   His influence upon the terrorists was the chief ground for his
obloquy; it was a significant commentary, however, upon the
conservatism of his earlier years that he was also assailed as a

royalist.   Parts of his *Plan de Constitution* with its mon-
archistic leanings were reprinted and spread broadcast.   His
former friend and disciple Fréron had now become the leader
of the moderate youth—the *jeunesse dorée*—who spent much
of their time destroying the busts of Marat wherever they
were to be found.   On January 21, 1795, he was burned in
effigy in the yard of the Jacobin Club and the ashes thrown
down the Montmartre sewer, giving rise to the popular story
that his body suffered a similar fate.   His heart was taken
from its saintly repository and may perhaps have undergone
such a disgrace.   Finally on February 8, the Convention decreed that no one who had been dead less than ten years was
to have the honor of Pantheonization.   Accordingly, Marat's
body was taken from its second resting-place, just as that of
Mirabeau had been less than six months before, and transferred to the Cemetery of the Clercs de Sainte Genéviève
nearby.

His reputation as a bloodthirsty monster grew apace.
Since very few of his contemporaries who were favorably disposed to him wrote their memoirs, whereas Brissot, Madame
Roland, Lafayette, Louvet, Meillan, Barbaroux, Buzot, Pétion, Barère, and others of his enemies left voluminous ones,
the picture that prevailed of him was that which the latter
presented.   The popular historians of the Revolution, middle-
class champions such as Lamartine, Michelet, Thiers, Taine,
and Carlyle, have done much to perpetuate this presentation.
Only more recently have biographers been content to assign to
him merely human rather than diabolical attributes, although
some of them have tended to err in the other direction.
Villiaumé and Esquiros began the more sympathetic study
that has since been continued by Chevremont, Bougeart, Bax,
Aulard, Stephens, Kropotkin, Jaurès, and Mathiez—some of
them the most learned and profound students of the French
Revolution.   They have varied in their interpretations of

Marat from glorifying him as the greatest figure of the Revolution to pardoning him for mistaken fanaticism, but they have not resorted in any case to the easy libel of insanity and megalomaniac ambition.

Despite the prevalent portrayal of Marat as a fiendish ogre, every revolutionary movement of the nineteenth century has witnessed a renaissance of his influence. It was probably not without some knowledge of Marat's journals that the founders of the most ardent of the republican clubs during the Revolution of 1830 gave to their society the name of *Amis du Peuples*. In 1833 a republican named Havard, disappointed with the results of the Revolution of 1830, put out an edition of Marat's *Chains of Slavery*, which he considered the best plea against monarchical despotism that he could make. Heine testifies to the popularity of Marat's most sanguinary speeches among the workingmen of Paris before the tumults of 1848. Constant Hilbey, a radical publisher, placarded the streets of Paris in 1846 with advertisements that reprints of certain of Marat's works could be bought at all bookstores; Hilbey was arrested and sentenced to fifteen days' imprisonment and a fine of one hundred francs. During the Revolution of 1848 there was organized in Paris a club known as *Les Amis du Peuple de la Révolution;* and in England one of the leaders of the Chartist movement was George Julian Harvey, who regarded Marat as his ideal and frequently signed himself *Ami du Peuple*. During the period preliminary to the Revolution of 1870 Bougeart, one of the most capable of the biographers of Marat, was sentenced to prison for four months for his book; and Vermorel, who in 1869 had published a collection of a few works of Marat in order to refute Gambetta's remark that Marat was a demagogue, died on the barricades in the streets of Paris during the days of the Commune of 1871. In more recent years, among those who studied Marat's work fairly or favorably were the radicals

Kropotkin, Jaurès, and Bax. And in 1921 a fifth edition of a small volume by Stefanov presenting the life of Marat in a highly favorable light was published by the State Publishing House at Moscow. ✳ In other words, no great European revolutionary movement from the days of Babeuf, who freely acknowledged his debt to Marat, to those of Lenin and Trotski have been without the influence of the self-styled People's Friend.

Such then was the career of Jean Paul Marat, son of a teacher of languages, doctor to the body-guard of the Count of Artois, friend of the people, and Nemesis of the Girondins. It is a career that presents many curious contrasts. While a physician who devoted unremunerated years to the cause of pure science, he sold patent medicines; while a conservative seeking a title of nobility and preaching that a good king is the finest creation of a friendly Providence, he had urged a more equitable distribution of property; while a radical protesting against privileged orders and ruling aristocracies, he had favored a dictatorship; while a demagogue clamoring for hundreds and thousands of heads, he had exerted every effort to save three of the impeached Girondins; and while a hard and relentless pursuer of the enemies of the Revolution, he had met his death at the hands of one who had hoped to gain access to him because she claimed to be unhappy. The essence of true greatness—the ability to mould events—was not his; he was moulded by events. ~~Some are born to radicalism; Marat had radicalism thrust upon him.~~ Force of circumstances outside of his control alone had changed him from a well-paid, complacent servant of the nobility into the leading spirit of the popular movement of his time. ~~It was not a movement that he had created but one at the head of which he had placed himself after it already existed and had become vigorous.~~

Throughout it all he retained, amidst his fiery attacks and

denunciations, enough of the old conservative instinct to make him cling to the monarchy until it had itself lost all footing, and to make him distrust all popular enterprises unless they had leaders who stood above the populace. He knew the strength of the people and desired it to be employed in their own behalf, but lacked confidence in them. He was not a democrat. He loved the common folk but did not respect them, as one loves an erring and misguided child. The keynote of his whole revolutionary creed, therefore, had been his cry for the concentration of power in clubs, tribunal, dictator, committee. He wished to insure the people's welfare through the aid of others, to reach a radical end by conservative means. But the people of his day trusted and followed him, unable to examine the program he preached for the attention required by his passionate, volcanic, melodramatic personality. And that is why revolutionaries since his time have seen in him an apostle of freedom and a martyr of liberty, without sharing his distrust of the common people, without adopting his policy of the undemocratic concentration of power in the hands of one or very few at most. But whether to friend or foe, his devotion to the cause of revolution has counted for all, the details of his political theories for naught. Detached from that devotion and that cause, he may perhaps appear to be the homicidal maniac he has sometimes been depicted, but it is well to remember that the explosive atmosphere of revolutions generally tends to produce some plainspoken soul whose uncompromising sincerity, whatever its conscious or unconscious basis, recognizes no legitimate obstacle in the way of success for the cause he champions.

BIBLIOGRAPHY

Of the large number of books by and on Marat, this bibliography includes only the ones used in this study and but the more important of those. A more complete list will be found in the bibliographies enumerated below.

BIBLIOGRAPHIES

1. Chevremont, *Marat, Index du bibliophile et de l'amateur de peintures, gravures, etc.* (Paris, 1876). This is a large volume devoted entirely to the works on and by Marat and to the paintings, sculptures, etc. in which he figures. It contains a careful study of Marat's journals and their imitations and continuations, which has been followed in the present work almost entirely. Such studies are also to be found in the books of Bougeart and Brunet, listed below.

2. Hatin, *Bibliographie historique et critique de la presse périodique française ou Catalogue systématique et raisonné de tous les écrits périodiques de quelque valeur publiés ou ayant circulé en France depuis l'origine du journal jusqu'à nos jours, avec extraits, notes historiques, critiques et morales, indication de prix que les principaux journaux ont atteints dans les ventes publiques, etc.* (Paris, 1866). This contains valuable information on Marat's contemporaries. On Marat's journals it is incomplete.

3. Mention ought also to be made of Tuetey, *Répertoire général des sources manuscrits de l'histoire de Paris pendant la Révolution française* (11 vols., Paris, 1890–1914) and of

4. Tourneux, *Bibliographie de l'histoire de Paris pendant la Révolution française* (5 vols., Paris, 1890–1913). Both of these are invaluable to the student of the French Revolution.

5. For the preparation of this bibliography Burr, *Catalogue of the Historical Library of Andrew Dickson White* (vol. II, *French Revolution*, Ithaca, N. Y., 1894) has been used frequently.

MARAT'S WORKS

A. Manuscripts

1. Proposed revisions in the page margins of *Découvertes* . . . *sur le feu, l'électricité et la lumière* (Bibliothèque Nationale Fr. 14734).

2. Proposed revisions in the page margins of *Découvertes sur la lumière* (Bibliothèque Nationale Fr. Nouv. Acq. 309).

3. Letter to Rose-Roume de St. Laurent, August 12, 1783 (British Museum Egerton Ms., 23, f. 59).

4. Letter to Bochart de Sarron, not dated, contained in presentation copy of *Mémoires académiques ou nouvelles Découvertes sur la lumière* (British Museum C. 60, i. 4).

5. Letter to M. de la Métherie, March 10, 1788 (British Museum, Jure empt., 24,024, f. 77).

6. Papers on the trial of Marat, April 23–24, 1793 (Archives nationales W 1b 269).

7. Proposed revisions of about twenty-five issues of Marat's journals (Bibliothèque Nationale F. N. A. 310).

8. The Notes and Manuscripts Collection of François Chevremont on Marat (British Museum, bearing the case number M. K. 5).

9. Notes of R. C. H. Catterall.

10. Numbers 1–8 above have been described in more detail or quoted in full in Gottschalk, *Du Marat inédit* in the *Annales historiques de la Révolution française*, May–June 1926, pp. 209–216.

B.   Original Editions

1. *Essay on the Human Soul* (London, 1772). Printed anonymously.

2. *A Philosophical Essay on Man, Being an Attempt to Investigate the Principles and Laws of the Reciprocal Influence of the Soul on the Body* (2 vols. in one, London, 1773).

3. *The Chains of Slavery, a Work Wherein the Clandestine and Villainous Attempts of Princes to Ruin Liberty Are Pointed out, and the Dreadful Scenes of Despotism Disclosed, to Which Is Prefixed an Address to the Electors of Great Britain, in order to Draw Their Timely Attention to the Choice of Proper Representatives in the Next Parliament* (London, 1774).

4. *De l'homme, ou des principes et des lois de l'influence de l'âme sur le corps et du corps sur l'âme* (3 vols., Amsterdam, 1775–1776). This is the French edition of no. 2.

5. *Découvertes de M. Marat, Docteur en Médecine et Médecin des Gardes-du-Corps de Monseigneur le Comte d'Artois, sur le feu, l'électricité et la lumière, constatées par une suite d'expériences nouvelles qui viennent d'être vérifiées par Mm. les Commissaires de l'Académie des Sciences* (Paris, 1779).

6. *Recherches physiques sur le feu, par M. Marat, Docteur en Médecine et Médecin des Gardes-du-Corps de Monseigneur le Comte d'Artois* (Paris, 1780).

7. *Découvertes de M. Marat (Docteur en Médecine et Medicin des Gardes-du-Corps de Monseigneur le Comte d'Artois) sur la lumière; constatées par une suite d'expériences nouvelles qui ont été faites un très grand nombre de fois sous les yeux de MM. les Commissaires de l'Académie de Sciences* (London and Paris, 1780).

8. *Recherches physiques sur l'électricité* (Paris, 1782).

9. *Mémoire sur l'Électricité médicale, couronné le 6 Août 1783, par l'Académie Royale des Sciences, Belles-Lettres et Arts de Rouen* (Paris, 1784).

10. *Observations de M. l'Amateur Avec à M. l'Abbé Sans sur la nécessité indispensable d'avoir une théorie solide et lumineuse avant d'ouvrir boutique d'Électricité médicale. En Réponse à la lettre de M. l'Abbé Sans à M. Marat sur l'ÉLECTRICITÉ POSITIVE ET NEGATIVE publiée dans le No. 16 de l'ANNÉE LITTÉRAIRE* (Paris, 1785).

11. *Optique de Newton, traduction nouvelle, faite par M *** sur la dernière Edition originale, Ornée de vingt-une Planches, et approuvée par l'Académie royale de Sciences; Dédié au Roi, Par M. Beauzée, Éditeur de cet Ouvrage, l'un des Quarante de l'Académie Française; de l'Académie DELLA CRUSEA; des Académies royales de Rouen, de Metz, et d'Arras; Professeur émérite de l'école royale militaire, et Secrétaire-Interprète de Monseigneur le Comte d'Artois* (Paris, 1787).

12. *Œuvres de M. Marat* (Paris, 1788). This contains *Mémoires académiques, ou nouvelles découvertes sur la lumière, relatives aux points les plus importants de l'optique* (pp. 1–114); *Mémoire sur la prétendue différente refrangibilité des Rayons hétérogènes* (pp. 115–150); *Mémoire sur l'explication de l'Arc-en-ciel donnée par Newton: envoyé au Concours ouvert par la Société Royale des Sciences de Montpellier en Octobre 1786* (pp. 151–250); and *Mémoire sur les vrais*

causes des couleurs que presentent les lames de verre, les bulles d'eau de savon, et autres matières diaphanes extrèment minces. Ouvrage qui a remporté le Prix de l'Académie de Sciences, Belles-Lettres et Art de Rouen, le 2 Août 1786.

13. *Offrande à la Patrie, ou discours au Tiers État de France* (Paris, 1789).

14. *L'Offrande à la Patrie (supplément) ou discours au Tiers-État de France sur le plan d'opération que ses députés aux États généraux doivent se proposer; sur les vices du gouvernement, d'où résulte le malheur public; sur la lettre de convocation et sur le réglement qui y est annexé* (Paris, 1789).

15. *Le Moniteur patriote*, no. 1 [c. August 11, 1789].

16. *La Constitution ou projet de Déclaration des droits de l'homme et du citoyen, suivi d'un plan de constitution juste, sage et libre. Par l'auteur de l'*OFFRANDE À LA PATRIE (Paris 1789).

17. *L'Ami du peuple* began with a prospectus published early in September 1789. Its original title was *Le Publiciste parisien, journal politique, libre et impartial. Par une Société de patriotes, et rédigé par M. Marat, auteur de l'*OFFRANDE À LA PATRIE, *du* MONITEUR, *et du* PLAN DE CONSTITUTION, *etc.* It continued under this name from September 12 to September 16, 1789, when it took the title of *L'Ami du peuple, ou le Publiciste parisien, etc.* As the *Ami du peuple* it was published with several gaps and a few supplements until no. 685 of September 21, 1792. On September 25 appeared the first issue of

18. *Le Journal de la République française, par Marat, l'ami du peuple, Député à la Convention nationale.* It continued under this name until the Convention decreed that no deputy might be employed at the same time as both journalist and representative of the people. With no. 144 of March 14, 1793, therefore, Marat called his paper sometimes *Le Publiciste de la République française* and sometimes *Observations à mes Commettans.* With no. 164 the title became definitely

19. *Le Publiciste de la République française, par Marat, l'ami du peuple, député à la Convention, auteur de plusieurs ouvrages politiques.* With this title it lasted until no. 242 of July 14, 1793, the day after the assassination of the author.

20. *Lettre de M. Marat, Ami du Peuple, à M. Joly, avocat aux Conseils, membre et secrétaire de l'Assemblée générale de Représentans de la Commune et l'un des soixante Administrateurs de la Municipalité* (Paris, 1789).

21. *Dénonciation faite au Tribunal du Public par M. Marat, l'Ami du Peuple, contre M. Necker, premier Ministre des Finances* (Paris, 1789).

22. *Appel à la nation par J. P. Marat, L'Ami du peuple, citoyen du District des Cordeliers et auteur de plusieurs ouvrages patriotiques* [London? 1790].

23. *Lettre de M. Marat, l'Ami du peuple, contenant quelques réflexions sur l'ordre judiciaire* (London, 1790).

24. *Nouvelle Dénonciation de M. Marat, l'Ami du peuple, contre M. Necker, premier Ministre des Finances, ou Supplément à la Dénonciation d'un citoyen contre un agent de l'autorité* (London, 1790).

25. *Le Junius français, journal politique*, nos. 1–13, June 2, 1790 to June 24, 1790. The fourth and subsequent issues appeared as *Le Junius français, journal politique par Marat, auteur de l'*AMI DU PEUPLE.

26. *Lettre de M. Marat, l'Ami du peuple, à M. le Président de l'Assemblée nationale* (Paris, 1790). An appeal for aid against those who have usurped his name and journal during his absence in England.

27. *Plan de Législation criminelle, ouvrage dans lequel on traite des délits et des peines, de la force des preuves et des présomptions, et de la manière d'acquérir ces preuves et ces présomptions durant l'instruction de la procédure, de manière à ne blesser ni la justice, ni la liberté, et à concilier la douceur avec la certitude des chatimens, et l'humanité avec la sûreté de la société civile* (Paris, 1790).

28. *C'en est fait de nous* (Paris [July 26, 1790]).

29. *On nous endort, Prenons-y garde* (Paris [August 9, 1790]).

30. *C'est un beau rève, Gare au reveil* (Paris [August 26, 1790]).

31. *L'Affreux Reveil* (Paris [August 30, 1790]).

32. *Relation fidèle des malheureuses affaires de Nancy* (Paris [September 12, 1790]).

33. *Relation authentique de ce qui s'est passé à Nancy, addressée aux députés du Régiment du Roi à l'Assemblée nationale, par leurs camarades* (Paris [September 18, 1790]).

34. *Les Charlatans modernes ou lettres sur le Charlatanisme Académique, publiées par M. Marat, l'Ami du peuple* (Paris, 1791).

35. *Lettre de l'Ami du peuple, aux fédérés des Quatre-vingt-trois départements* [Paris, August 9, 1792]. This is an appeal to the people of France to make prisoners of the royal household.

36. *Marat, l'Ami du peuple, à ses concitoyens les électeurs* [Paris,

September 1792]. A reply to the campaign attacks of his opponents.

37. *Opinion de Marat, l'Ami du Peuple, Député à la Convention nationale, sur le jugement de l'ex-monarque, imprimée par ordre de la Convention* (Paris [1792]).

38. *Discours de Marat, l'Ami du Peuple, sur la défense de Louis XVI, la conduite à tenir par la Convention, et la marche alarmante que la faction royaliste s'efforce de lui faire dans le jugement du tyran détroné* (Paris [1792]).

39. *Les Chaines de l'Esclavage, ouvrage destiné à developper les noirs attentats des princes contre les peuples; les ressorts secrets, les ruses, les menées, les artifices, les coups d'état qu'ils employent pour détruire la liberté, les scènes sanglantes qui accompagnent le despotisme* (Paris, *l'an premier de la République* [1793]).

40. *Profession de Foi de Marat, l' Ami du peuple, député à la Convention, addressée au peuple français en général et à ses commettans en particulier* (Paris [March 30, 1793]).

41. *Société des Amis de la Liberté et de l'Égalité, séante aux ci-devant Jacobins, Saint Honoré, à Paris. Lettre de Marat aux Jacobins.* [Paris, April 1793]. Contains a letter of Marat (April 15, 1793) asking for their protection and support, and another (April 19, 1793) in which he enclosed his letters of April 17 to the Convention denouncing the Girondins.

42. *Société des Amis de la Liberté et de l'Égalité, séante aux ci-devant Jacobins* (Paris, June 21, 1793). This is Marat's last letter to the Jacobins, explaining his attitude on the dictatorship, printed by order of the Society.

C. Posthumous Editions and Redactions

1. *Plan de Législation criminelle par Marat, l'Ami du peuple. . . . De l'imprimerie de la Veuve Marat.* (Paris, 1793). Chevremont calls this "*la plus rare de toutes les editions.*"

2. *Les Chaines de l'Esclavage, ouvrage destiné, etc. . . . Précédées d'un discours préliminaire et accompagnées de nouvelles notes par M. A. Havard* (Paris, 1833).

3. *Marat et son éditeur, Constant Hilbey, devant la Cour d'assises, relation du procès et suivie de nouveaux extraits de l'*AMI DU PEUPLE (Paris, 1847).

4. *Un Roman de Cœur, par Marat, l'Ami du Peuple, publié pour la première fois, en son entier, d'après le manuscript autographe et

précédé d'une notice littéraire, par le bibliophile Jacob (2 vols., in one, Paris, 1848).

5. *Le Sang de Marat. Fac-simile des numeros 506 et 678 du Journal l'*AMI DU PEUPLE *teints du sang de Marat, donnés par Albertine Marat, sa sœur, au Colonel Maurin, communiqués par M. Anatole France. . . . Notice par M. Chéron de Villiers* (Paris, 1865).

6. *Œuvres de Marat* (*l'Ami du Peuple*) *receuillies et annotées par A. Vermorel* (Paris, 1869).

7. *Placards de Marat, l'Ami du Peuple, par F. Chevremont, le bibliographe de Marat* (Paris, 1877).

8. *Eloge de Montesquieu, présenté à l'Académie de Bordeaux le 28 Mars 1785 par J. P. Marat, publié avec une Introduction par Arthur de Brezetz* (Libourne, 1887).

9. *Reprint of the Two Tracts, 1. An Essay on Gleets, 2. An Enquiry into the Nature, Cause, and Cure of a Singular Disease of the Eyes, by Jean Paul Marat, M.D., edited with an introduction by James Blake Bailey, Librarian of the Royal College of Surgeons of England* (London, 1891).

10. *De la Presbytie Accidentelle par J. P. Marat Docteur en Médecine* (*1776*), *traduit pour la première fois de l'Anglais d'après le seul exemplaire connu, appartenant à la Bibliothèque de la Société royale de Médecine et de Chirurgie de Londres par Georges Pilotelle, précédé d'une introduction par le bibliographe de Marat* (Paris, 1891). This is a translation of no. 2 of the *Reprint of Two Tracts.*

11. *Marat, l'Ami du Peuple, aux Braves Parisiens, 26 Août, 1792, huitième placard réédité pour la première fois par Georges Pilotelle, et précédé d'une notice historique par le bibliographe de Marat* (London and Paris, 1892).

12. *Polish Letters, by Jean Paul Marat, translated from the original unpublished manuscript, issued by the Bibliophile Society for Members only* (2 vols., Boston, 1904).

13. Vellay, *Les Pamphlets de Marat, avec une introduction et des notes* (Paris, 1911).

14. Simond, *Marat, Autographe de Marat, les Chaînes de l'Esclavage, Plan de législation criminelle, l'Ami du Peuple, Journal de la République française, Biographie, Bibliographie, Choix de textes* (Paris [1911]). This book is made up largely of selections from the works mentioned. The biographical and bibliographical sketches are indifferent.

D. Correspondence

1. Vellay, *La Correspondance de Marat* (Paris, 1908).

2. Vellay, *Supplément à la Correspondance de Marat, extrait de la*
REVUE DE LA REVOLUTION FRANÇAISE, *Janvier-Mars 1910, pp. 81–95,
Avril-Juin, pp. 219–235.*

3. Vellay, *Lettres inédites de Marat à Benjamin Franklin* in the
Revue historique de la Révolution française, vol. III, 1912, pp. 353–
361. This article contains ten letters of Marat to Franklin asking him
for opinions, inviting him to attend his demonstrations, etc.

4. Payenneville, *Deux Lettres inédites de Marat* in the *Revue
historique de la Révolution française*, vol. XVI, 1919–1922, pp.
190–202.

5. A letter in *Notes and Queries*, 12 S, XI, July 15, 1922, p. 53
by Andrew de Ternant speaking of two letters of Marat, which are
probably not authentic.

E. Addresses

1. For the speeches of Marat, any of the contemporary newspapers
that reported the debates of the Convention is good. Reference in this
study is made to either the *Archives Parlementaires de 1787 à 1860,
recueil complet des débats législatifs et politiques des Chambres
françaises, imprimé par ordre du Senat et de la Chambre des Députés, première série 1787 à 1799* (Paris 1867– , 82 vols. to date)
or to

2. *Le Moniteur universel.* The author has been able to use both
the original of this paper, known as the *Gazette nationale, ou le
Moniteur universel* (21 vols., Paris, 1789–1799) and the reprint,
known as the *Réimpression de l'ancien Moniteur* (30 vols., Paris 1843–
1845). These speeches have always been compared with the quotations
from them contained in Marat's journals. Where the latter have
differed from those of the *Archives parlementaires* and the *Moniteur*,
they have always been quoted, on the assumption that the written
word will express one's ideas more clearly and accurately than the
spoken. Seldom have Marat's addresses, as he quoted them in his
papers, differed greatly from those he actually delivered—and then
only in phraseology, never in thought.

3. For Marat's addresses at the Club of the Jacobins, see Aulard,

La Société des Jacobins, Recueil de documents pour l'histoire du Club des Jacobins de Paris (6 vols., Paris, 1889).

OTHER PRIMARY SOURCES

A. Memoirs

1. *Portrait de Marat par P. F. N. Fabre D'Églantine, représentant du peuple, Député de Paris à la Convention Nationale* (Paris, seconde année de la République).

2. Maton de la Varenne, *Les Crimes de Marat et des autres égorgeurs; Ma Résurrection où parmi quelques matériaux précieux pour l'histoire on trouve la preuve que Marat et d'autres scélérats, membres des Autorités publiques, ont provoqué tous les massacres des prisonniers* (2nd edition, Paris, 1795).

3. Madame Roland de la Platière, *Appel à l'impartiale postérité: recueil des écrits qu'elle a rédigés pendant sa détention aux prisons de l'Abbaye et de Saint-Pélagie* (4 parts in 1 vol., Paris [1795]).

4. *Mémoires de Meillan, Député pour le Département des Basses-Pyrénées à la Convention nationale, avec des notes et des éclaircissements historiques* (Paris, 1823).

5. Barbaroux, *Mémoires* (3rd edition, Paris, 1827).

6. *Mémoires de Brissot, Membre de l'Assemblée législative et de la Convention nationale, sur les contemporains et la Révolution française, publiés par son fils avec des notes et des éclaircissements historiques par M. F. de Montrol* (4 vols., Paris, 1830).

7. Lafayette, *Mémoires, Correspondance, et Manuscrits, publiés par sa famille* (6 vols., Paris, 1837–1838).

8. *Mémoires inédits de Pétion et mémoires de Buzot et de Barbaroux, accompagnés de notes inédites de Buzot et de nombreux documents inédits sur Barbaroux, Buzot, Brissot, etc., précédés d'une introduction par C. A. Dauban* (Paris, 1866).

9. *Mémoires de Barras, membre du Directoire, publiés avec une introduction générale, des préfaces et des appendices, par Georges Duruy* (Paris, 1895).

B. Other Contemporary Sources

1. Desmoulins, *Révolutions de France et de Brabant* (104 nos. in 8 vols., Paris, 1789–1791).

2. Prudhomme, *Révolutions de Paris* (225 nos. in 17 vols., Paris, 1789–1794).

3. *Pièces justificatives relativement à l'exécution d'un Décret lancé contre le sieur Marat* (Paris, 1790). This is a statement of the District of the Cordeliers which presents its side of the Marat Affair.

4. *Dénonciation à l'Assemblée nationale de deux imprimés ayant pour titre l'un:* c'en est fait de nous *et l'autre:* révolutions de france et de brabant, *par Malouet, député d'Auvergne, séance du 31 juillet* (Paris, 1790).

5. *Ni Roland ni Marat, opinion d' Anacharsis Cloots, député du Département de l'Oise à la Convention nationale* (Paris, 1792).

6. *Appel nominal qui a eu lieu dans la séance permanente du 13 au 14 avril, 1793, l'an deuxième de la République française, à la suite du rapport du Comité de Législation, sur la question: Y-a-t-il lieu d'accusation contre Marat, Membre de la Convention nationale? Imprimé par ordre de la Convention nationale et envoyé à tous les Départements et aux Armées* (Paris [April 1793]).

7. *Bulletin du Tribunal criminel révolutionnaire établi au Palais à Paris par la loi du 10 Mars 1793, pour juger sans appel les conspirateurs.* Nos. 16–18 contain the record of Marat's trial.

8. *Oraison funèbre de Marat, l'Ami du Peuple, prononcée par le citoyen F. E. Guiraut* (Paris, 1793). This is chosen for special mention from among many such orations because it gives a short sketch of Marat's life and indicates to what an extent his career was known and appreciated by his contemporaries.

9. *Apothéose de Marat et Lepeletier à Versailles* (Paris, 1793). This is a collection of sixteen pages of poems dedicated to Marat and Lepeletier.

10. Vatel, *Procès criminel de Charlotte de Corday devant le Tribunal révolutionnaire* (Paris, 1861).

11. *Œuvres politiques de Marat, l'Ami du peuple. Prospectus.* Announcing the intention of the Veuve Marat to publish his complete works in eight volumes. The plan was suppressed.

12. *La Dépanthéonization de Jean Paul Marat, Patron des Hommes de sang et des Terroristes, Fondée sur ses crimes et sur les forfaits des Jacobins. Par Henriquez, Citoyen de la Section du Panthéon français* (Paris, n. d. but of 1795).

SECONDARY SOURCES

A. General Histories

1. The classical histories of the French Revolution by Michelet (7 vols., Paris, 1847–1853), Mignet (10th edition, 2 vols., Paris, 1869), Quinet (2 vols., 6th edition, Paris, 1869), Blanc (12 vols., Paris, 1847–1862), Thiers (4 vols., New York, 1866), Taine (3 vols., Paris, 1878–1885), Carlyle (3 vols., London, 1842), and Von Sybel (4 vols., London, 1867–1869), all may be treated together, since they give an impression of Marat that is more or less biased and unjust. The worst in this respect are Carlyle and Michelet, and the best Mignet and Von Sybel.

2. Buchez and Roux, *Histoire parlementaire de la Révolution française, ou journal des Assemblées nationales 1789–1815* (40 vols., Paris, 1834–1838). This is made up almost entirely of portions of the proceedings of the various legislative bodies, the popular societies, the Commune, and of other contemporary documents.

3. Esquiros, *Histoire des Montagnards* (2 vols., Paris, 1847). The author of this work claims to have based his story of Marat upon notes furnished him by Albertine, the sister of Marat. His work is, however, extremely melodramatic and sometimes highly imaginative. It is favorable to Marat.

4. Villiaumé, *Histoire de la Révolution française* (6th edition, 3 vols., Paris, 1864). This was one of the first books to attempt an apology for Marat. This author too was able to consult Marat's own notes and papers. It is inexact and biased.

5. Lamartine, *Histoire des Girondins* (4 vols., Paris, 1858). This is an entirely inaccurate and untrustworthy account as far as it deals with Marat. Lamartine knew his sources, but adapted them in language and content to suit his own purposes. His aim being to glorify the Girondins, naturally he makes Marat out to have been a sort of demon.

6. Hatin, *Histoire politique et littéraire de la presse en France avec une introduction historique sur les origines du journal et la bibliographie générale des journaux depuis leur origine* (8 vols., Paris, 1859–1861). This contains (Vol VI) a long biography of Marat, emphasizing his journalistic influence. It is the "standard" history of French journalism.

7. Mortimer-Ternaux, *Histoire de la Terreur 1792–1794* (8 vols., Paris, 1862–1881). This work is more of a history of the French Revolution from 1789 to 1794 than its title implies. The author is a partisan of the Gironde and therefore hostile to Marat. The book is a mine of information and contains many valuable documents, otherwise not easily accessible, in its appendices.

8. Dauban, *La Démagogie en 1793 à Paris, ou Histoire jour par jour de l'année 1793, accompagnée de documents contemporains rares ou inédits* (Paris, 1868). This contains large extracts from several rare sources. It is bitterly opposed, as the title would suggest, to Marat and his colleagues of the Mountain.

9. Stephens, *The French Revolution* (2 vols., New York, 1886–1891) devotes a large amount of space to Marat. He is friendly to Marat but is sometimes inaccurate.

10. Charavay, *Assemblées électorales de Paris* (3 vols., Paris, 1890). This is the best source of information on the part Marat played in the Paris electoral assemblies.

11. Lacroix, *Actes de la Commune de Paris pendant la Révolution* (2 series, 8 vols. in each, Paris, 1894–1898). This is a good source of knowledge on the attitude of the early Commune toward Marat. It does not extend far enough to be of use on his influence in 1792–1793.

12. *Histoire Socialiste 1789–1900* (edited by Jaurès, 13 vols., Paris [1900–1909]). The three volumes on the Revolution are by Jaurès himself and contain by far the best discussion on the socialist inclinations of Marat.

13. Kropotkin, *The Great French Revolution 1789–1793* (translated from the French by N. F. Dryhurst, New York, 1909). This is based largely upon Jaurès's history, but is more favorable to Marat.

14. Acton, *Lectures on the French Revolution* (London, 1910). Lord Acton's sentimental sympathy for Charlotte Corday mars an otherwise severe but accurate portrayal of her victim.

15. Aulard, *Histoire politique de la Révolution française* (Paris, 1901) and the translation of this by Bernard Miall (*The French Revolution: A Political History*, 4 vols., New York, 1910). This presents a splendid account of the development of republicanism in France and pays considerable attention to Marat. The translation is inaccurately rendered and contains a short biographical sketch of

Marat by the translator which is little more than a collection of the most unsavory legends regarding him.

16. Aulard, *Études et Leçons sur la Révolution française*, vol. II, pp. 39–106 (Paris, 1902) is one of the best accounts of the responsibility for the September Massacres.

17. Mathiez, *Le Club des Cordeliers pendant la crise de Varennes et la Massacre du Champ de Mars* (Paris, 1910). Marat receives only scant notice here, but it is the best monograph we have on his relations with the Cordeliers, though for but a short period.

18. *Histoire de France contemporaine depuis la Révolution jusqu'à la Paix de 1919* (edited by Lavisse, 10 vols., Paris, 1920–1922). Volumes I and II are by Sagnac and Pariset respectively. They cover the period during which Marat was active. Their discussion of him is entirely factual and accurate.

19. Cünow, *Die revolutionäre Zeitungsliteratur Frankreichs während der Jahre 1789–1794* (Berlin, 1908). An account of journalism during the first years of the Revolution which devotes a large chapter to the work of Marat. Favorably disposed.

20. Stephens, *Women of the French Revolution* (New York, 1922) contains good accounts of Simonne Evrard and Charlotte Corday, and of Marat's influence on women's organizations.

21. Braesch, *La Commune du dix août 1792, Étude sur l'histoire de Paris du 20 juin au 2 decembre 1792* (Paris, 1911) is a long, detailed study of a short period, giving Marat a considerable amount of unfriendly attention in an endeavor to prove the Committee of Surveillance responsible for the September Massacres.

22. Gibbs, *Men and Women of the French Revolution* (London, 1906). Chapter VI, entitled *The People's Friend*, is a brief account of the life of Marat.

23. McLaurin, *Post Mortem: Essays Historical and Medical* (New York, 1923) contains (pp. 191–203) a sketch of Marat's career which is based upon only the most meagre knowledge. It is an attempt to be scientific which succeeds only in being ridiculous.

24. Mathiez, *La Révolution française*. Only two volumes (Paris, 1922–1924) have thus far appeared, but these cover the period of the Revolution down to the Fall of the Girondins. The author's well known Montagnard sympathies have caused him to give more than the usual amount of space to Marat and with more understanding than has ever been done before in a general history.

B. Biographies

1. Brunet, *Marat, dit l'Ami du Peuple, notice sur sa vie et ses ouvrages* (Paris, 1862) is a fair account of Marat, unfortunately too short.

2. Bougeart, *Marat l'Ami du Peuple* (2 vols., Paris, 1865). This is the best biography of Marat yet written. It is, however, blindly favorable to him, even to the point of quoting—at least in one case— in an order not strictly chronological, so as to lead to conclusions that are not entirely true.

3. Chéron de Villiers, *Marie-Anne-Charlotte de Corday d'Armont* (Paris, 1865) is good on the death and funeral of Marat, but unfavorably biased on his career.

4. Fassey, *Marat, sa mort, ses véritables funérailles, d'après les documents empruntés aux archives de la Préfecture de Police* (Paris, 1867) is the best account of the death, funeral, cult, Pantheonization and depantheonization of Marat, though it is inclined to be overfavorable to him.

5. *Marat ou les Héros de la Révolution (Grand Roman National Historique) par Leo Taxil et J. Vindex* (Paris, n. d.). A panegyric novel, not badly informed.

6. Chevremont, *Jean Paul Marat, esprit politique, accompagné de sa vie scientifique, politique et privée* (2 vols., Paris, 1880). This is neither a biography of Marat nor a study of his political philosophy, as it claims to be, but rather a splendid collection of sources arranged in chronological order with connecting comment and narrative. As is to be expected of a man who devoted almost an entire lifetime to the study of another, Chevremont is inclined to regard Marat with great love and reverence.

7. Beesly, *Life of Danton* (London, 1889) is a good account of the associations of Marat and Danton, but a better is

8. Madelin, *Danton* (translated by Lady Mary Loyd, New York, 1921). This is the best and most recent account of Danton. Madelin is not in sympathy with the French Revolutionary movement and therefore presents Marat in the traditional manner.

9. Belloc, *Robespierre* (New York, 1901) is the best biography of Robespierre in English and therefore the best for a presentation of the relations of the two men from the Robespierre point of view. The

same hostile spirit as is to be found in the author's *Danton* (New York, 1899) toward Marat mars this account also.

10. Bax, *Jean Paul Marat, the People's Friend* (Boston, 1901). This is the best work in English on Marat, but is given to hero-worship. It seems to be based almost exclusively upon the two volumes of Bougeart.

11. Cabanès, *Marat inconnu, l'homme privé, le médecin, le savant, d'après des documents nouveaux et inédits* (2nd edition, Paris [1911]). This is a very good narrative of the life of Marat before the Revolution. It presents a careful estimate of his scientific work and is good in general for moot points in his career. The legends of his having been a thief, horse-leech, etc. receive conclusively destructive attention.

12. Gottschalk, *The Tragedy of Marat* (Girard, Kansas, 1923). A brief summary of Marat's career intended for popular consumption.

C. Periodical Literature

1. Bowen-Graves, *Marat* in the *Fortnightly Review*, XXI, February 1874, pp. 43–74. This is a good short summary of Marat's life, somewhat apologetic for him.

2. Bax, *Jean Paul Marat* in the *Gentleman's Magazine*, New Series, XIX, November 1877, pp. 572–593, is an exact study, suffering, like the author's larger work, from hero-worship.

3. Stephens, *Marat the Friend of the People* in the *Pall Mall Magazine*, X, no. 41, 1896, gives a good short biography of Marat.

4. Roberts, *Marat as an Englishman* in the *Gentleman's Magazine*, May 1900, disproves the stories sometimes told of Marat's criminal proclivities in England.

5. Gunther, *Jean Paul Marat, der "Ami du Peuple" als Criminalist* in *Der Gerichtssaal*, LXI, 1902, nos. 3–6, discusses at great length with frequent quotations the criminology of Marat's *Plan de législation criminelle*.

6. Babut, *Une journée au District des Cordeliers* in the *Revue historique*, March–April 1903. This is the story of the attempt to arrest Marat on January 22, 1790, based upon the testimony of eye-witnesses.

7. Matouchet, *Le Mouvement électorale à Paris* in the *Révolution*

française, XLIV, 1903, pp. 227–234, quotes long passages advocating the election of Marat to the Convention.

8. Catterall, *The Credibility of Marat* in the *American Historical Review*, XVI, 1910–1911, is an analysis of Marat's story of the composition and publication of the *Chains of Slavery*. Professor Catterall shows convincingly that Marat exaggerated the facts in this particular instance, but his conclusion that Marat's statements are always unreliable is far too sweeping.

9. Chuquet, *L'Assassinat de Marat* in *Séances et Travaux, Institut de France, Académie des sciences morales et politiques*, new series, vol. 88, 1917. A detailed study of Charlotte Corday's acts on July 13, 1793.

10. Gottschalk, *The Radicalism of Jean Paul Marat* in the *Sewanee Review*, April 1921, is an account of the development of republicanism in Marat.

11. Mathiez, *La Mort de Marat et le vote de la loi sur l'accaparement* in *Annales révolutionnaires*, November–December 1921, XIII, pp. 477–489 is a study of the influence of Marat and his assassination upon the food laws of July–September 1793.

12. Gottschalk, *Marat dans la journée du 14 juillet 1789* in *La Révolution française*, January–March 1923, XVII, pp. 13–18 is an analysis of the part Marat played in the Fall of the Bastille.

13. Gottschalk, *The Criminality of Jean Paul Marat* in *The South Atlantic Quarterly*, April 1926, pp. 154–167. This is a reply to Phipson's *Jean Paul Marat: His Career in England and France before the Revolution* (London, 1924). Phipson revives all of the long discarded stories regarding the lowliness of the life that Marat led in England and France before 1789. This article tries not only to disprove the charges made against Marat but to discover how the legend came into existence.

SUPPLEMENTARY BIBLIOGRAPHY (1967)

For some leading titles that appeared between 1927 and 1936, see my "Quelques études récentes sur Marat," cited on p. v n. 1, above.

SELECTED TITLES PUBLISHED SINCE 1936

A. Biographies of Marat

1. Z. Friedland, *Zhan-Pol Marat i Grazhdanskaia Voina XVIII v.* (2nd ed.; Moscow, 1959). If allowance be made for "the party line," it must be considered the most serious recent study of the subject.

2. Jean Massin, *Marat* (Paris, 1960). Probably the best of several recent accounts in French. Has a perceptive bibliography (pp. 299–303).

B. Monographs on Related Subjects

1. Albert Mathiez, *La Révolution française*, Vol. III (Paris, 1927) completes the history mentioned above (p. 209). The three volumes have been translated into English and published as one volume (New York, 1928).

2. Pierre Caron, *Les massacres de Septembre* (Paris, 1935) scrutinizes the numerous documents on the massacres before and after those in Paris in September 1792 and comes to much the same conclusions (see especially pp. 168, n. 8, 189–91, 286, n. 2, and 297–300) as that given above (pp. 120–28) regarding Marat's role.

3. J. M. Thompson, *Robespierre* (2 vols.; Oxford, 1935) replaces Belloc's work (see p. 210 above) as the best biography of Robespierre in English.

4. Hugo Rozbroj, *Jean-Paul Marat (1743–93). Ein Naturforscher und Revolutionär, sein Zusammentreffen in der Geisteswelt mit Goethe, Lamarck, Rousseau u. a.* (Berlin, 1937). Considers Marat's work as a scientist worthy of more respectful attention than it has generally received.

5. Georges Lefebvre, *La Révolution française* (Paris, 1951) has been translated into English in two volumes (New York, 1962 and 1964). It is generally considered the best recent study of the French Revolution (to 1799).

6. M. J. Sydenham, *The Girondins* (London, 1961) ably presents the widely accepted view (which, however, Marat probably would not have accepted) that the Girondins were too loosely associated to constitute a faction or a party.

7. Friedrich Lohmann, *Jean Paul Marat und das Strafrecht in der französischen Revolution* (Bonn, 1963). An analysis of Marat's ideas on criminal law reform and their effect.

8. Alfred Cobban, *The Social Interpretation of the French Revolution* (Cambridge, England, 1964). Argues (perhaps somewhat superfluously) against the interpretation of the French Revolution as a struggle of the industrial bourgeoisie against the landed aristocracy.

C. Some Relevant Articles

1. René Farge, "Le local du Club des Cordeliers et le cœur de Marat," *Annales historiques de la Révolution française*, IV (1927), 320–47.

2. A. Soboul, "Sentiments religieux et cultes populaires," *Annales historiques de la Révolution française*, XXIX (1957), 193–213. Describes the cult of Marat at some length.

3. V. M. Daline, "Babeuf et Marat en 1789–1790," *Annales historiques de la Révolution française*, XXX (1958), 16–37. Shows that the relations of Babeuf with Marat in the early stages of the Revolution were closer than hitherto believed.

4. Emile Mara, "L'origine et l'ame sardes de Jean-Paul Mara, dit Marat," *Annales historiques de la Révolution française*, XXXVI (1964), 78–84. On the Mara family of Sardinia.

APPENDIX

The following letter of Augustin, the brother of Maximilien Robespierre, to his friend Buissart is of great interest and significance, and should be read in connection with the events described on pp. 167–170 and 185–186. It has recently been published in Michon, *Correspondance de Maximilien et Augustin Robespierre* (Paris, 1926), pp. 174–175:

Paris, July 15, 1793.

Nothing extraordinary here. The troublesome events that we were to fear for today have not taken place. It is to be hoped that the schemers will not succeed this time in their plots. A panic of terror seizes many souls and the crowds at the bakers' are considerable. The death of Marat will probably be useful to the Republic by the circumstances that accompany it. She is a *ci-devant*, come from Caen designedly, sent by Barbaroux and other rascals, first directed to a member of the Right at Paris, to that fanatic Duperrey [*sic*] who twice drew his sword in the Assembly and threatened Marat several times. We have decreed him "of accusation" as an accomplice of the assassin. You will see in the newspapers the details of this affair and it will not be difficult to judge the men with whom we have to deal. The Minister of the Interior has, it appears, been designated to the sword of this monstrous woman who has made Marat fall under her blows. Danton, Maximilien are still threatened. A remarkable thing is the means that this infernal female used to gain access to our colleague. Although Marat has been depicted as a monster of a type so terrible that all France is deceived into believing that there is no cannibal comparable to this citizen, this woman, nevertheless, implores his commiseration. She writes him: "It is enough to be unhappy to be heard." This circumstance is well calculated to demaratize Marat and to open the eyes of those who in good faith believe us sanguinary men. You must know that Marat lived like a Spartan, that he spent nothing on himself, and that he gave everything he had to those who had recourse to him. Several times he said to me and

215

to my colleagues: "I have nothing more to give to help the unfortunate crowd that appeal to me. I will send some of them to you," and he did so several times.

Judge for yourself our political situation, a situation brought about by scandals. Some patriots, ardent but not very enlightened, are at this moment in accord with the conspirators to Pantheonize Marat.

The circumstances are such that this proposal may perpetuate these scandals; that hatred, which seems to desert corpses, will stick to Marat in the grave; and that the system of the enemies of liberty will take on more strength than if our colleague were still among us. The most skilful observer would be astonished that the most terrible weapon of the enemies of liberty is scandal. He would groan at the ignorance and credulity of a people that always fails to recognize it. Any scandal, no matter how absurd, will thrive, and Paris, which sees its most ardent defenders slaughtered and is content to shed tears upon their graves, will still have to defend itself for centuries against detractors, while Evreux, Caen, Lyons, Marseilles will enjoy an almost immortal glory, because those cities will have as defenders the most skilful of the conspirators, the most criminal of men.

SUPPLEMENTARY APPENDIX (1967)

Two Questions Answered

A letter to the editor of the *Manchester Guardian*, published on August 10, 1957, has been called to my attention by Professor Raymond O. Rockwood, Colgate University. Written by George A. Carter, Chief Librarian of the Municipal Library of Warrington, it stated that he had found under date of September 10, 1771, an item in the accounts of the Warrington Academy which recorded a payment of £3.3s. to "Mr. Mara for journey" (as well as two entries is 1772 for a "French Master"). The "Mr. Mara" thus mentioned in 1771 may or may not have been the "French Master" mentioned in 1772, and he may or may not have been Jean Paul Marat. In any case, it now seems clear that the prisoner in the Bristol jail (see pp. 6-8 above) could not have been Marat. In a recent article Robert Darnton quotes a hitherto unknown letter written by Marat from Geneva on May 14, 1776.[1] If the letter is authentic, and there is every reason to believe that it is, it should dispose definitively of the contention that Marat was in prison as a thief in the British Isles from roughly March 1776 to June 1777. Even without this piece of evidence other scholars had tended toward the same conclusion.[2]

A different sort of question about Marat's later career was answered some years ago by the turning up of another piece

[1] "Marat n'a pas été un voleur: Une lettre inédite," *Annales historiques de la Revolution française*, **XXXVIII** (1966), 447–50.

[2] J. M. Thompson, "Le Maitre, alias Mara," *English Historical Review*, **XLIX** (1934), 55–73, carefully compiled all the evidence incriminating Marat he could find but concluded, somewhat reluctantly, that "the impartial historian can only record a verdict of 'Not Proven'" (p. 73). And H. McLachlin, *Warrington Academy, Its History and Influence* (Manchester, 1943), pp. 77–80, readily concurred.

of documentary evidence. The Noel Charavay catalogue of autographs, sale of January 26–28, 1932, offered as item 376 Marat's original letter of resignation, addressed to the Committee of Public Safety, Paris, June 2, 1793. It reads: "I relinquish the exercise of my functions as deputy until after the trial of the accused representatives." This wording makes clear that the resignation mentioned on p. 166 above was provisional and probably explains why no attention was paid to it.

INDEX

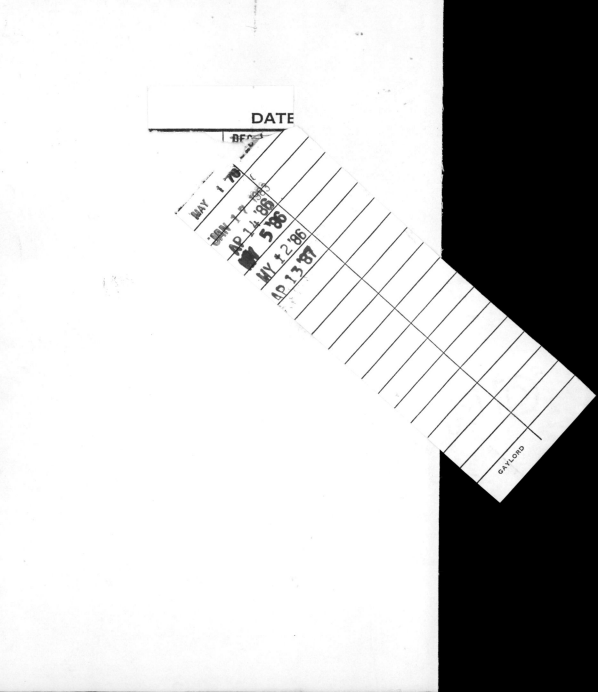

DATE

MAY 1 70

MAY 1 2

AP 14 '86

5 '86

MY 2 '86

MY 13 87

AP 13 87

GAYLORD